HEART OF WORSHIP

theheartofworship.net

HEART OF WORSHIP

31 DAILY THOUGHTS TO NOURISH THE HEART OF A WORSHIPER

Cover design and copy layout by Savannah Sullivan
Editors: Pam Nolde. James Roberts. Nanci Holston. Laura Payne. Carene Bracken

---

This collection of devotions comes from the heart of
31 gifted writers who are part of the
Heart of Worship Kingdom Community.
Some have been speakers.
Some are part of our band or frontline team.
Others are part of our prayer or administrative team.

Each one has traveled a unique journey that has
shaped the wisdom and the insight they are sharing.
God has allowed us to be "fitly joined together"
so that His Kingdom can be blessed.
This book would not be what it is without their contributions.
We celebrate the wonder of living in Kingdom Community.

TABLE OF CONTENTS

con't

DEDICATION

In the early 2000's, in a prayer meeting prior to our annual
Heart of Worship conference, God gave me a vision. I saw a giant wall.
On my side of the wall stood a few of the HOW leadership.

From a bird's eye view, I saw what was on the other side.
It was a sea of people stretching far.
And they were waiting. Just waiting.

Suddenly we began to tear down the wall. Piece by piece.
At first we could only see glimpses of the crowd
through the holes we were making.
But then the wall began to fall and we were caught in the rubble.
It was then something truly amazing happened.
The worshipers that had been standing immobile
on the other side began to flood over us.
They poured out with energy and anticipation.
They began to sing and praise God.

And I felt the Lord say to me,
"The mission of Heart of Worship Ministries
is to release the worshipers."

This devotional is another step in our journey.
The words on these pages are intended to
release worshipers from fear, worry and insecurity.
With personal stories and insights,
we instead release confidence, courage and joy
over your ministries.

So this book is dedicated to YOU.
Dedicated to every worshiper seeking to
authentically flood the earth with the beautiful sound of your praise.
You are why this ministry exists.
These devotions are for you.

Laura Payne, Heart of Worship Ministries founder

GUARDING THE WONDER

1

WONDER | KEVIN HOWARD

Kevin is a member of the HOW steering team. His musical excellence and nurturing spirit has made him a mentor to hundreds. He is a sought-after clinician whose influence is felt among Apostolics around the globe.

> *On the glorious splendor of your majesty,*
> *and on your wonderful works I will meditate.*
> *(Psalm 145:5) ESV*

> *Listen to this, Job; stop and consider God's wonders.*
> *(Job 37:14) ESV*

> *As soon as all the people saw Jesus,*
> *they were overwhelmed with wonder and ran to greet him.*
> *(Mark 9:15) NIV*

Have you ever considered why children ask multiple questions every day? And why, sometimes, their favorite word is "why"? They are inquisitive about everything. Sometimes it can reach a level of pure annoyance.

A couple of years ago, I remember sitting on a plane in front of a mother and small child. Every few seconds, the young girl would say, "Mommy, what is this for?" referring to the arm rest…then "Why is the window round?" and so on for the entire trip. I could hear the exasperation in the mom's voice growing with each question.

I mused about the little girl's seemingly endless list of questions and realized that as an adult, I don't think to ask very many questions. Why not? Have I really learned everything there is to know in life? Could it be I don't have near the capacity for wonder I once did as a child? Does so much of life crowd me that I basically turn my attention to what I know and just keep it there? Do I really not care enough to question something or learn something new?

Every day is a gift from the hand of God. A day full of possible challenges and hardships, yes, but also of great potential, exploration and discovery. God has given us His wonderful creation to enjoy. He has put His creative nature in us to find unique ways to express His amazing glory and grace. In the midst of every season of life, He gives us the ability and a chance to express in many ways how amazing He truly is.

I believe the issue of wonder all comes down to our perspective. Do I see God as big? Do I see myself as fearfully and wonderfully made? Do I have a grateful heart and see all He has done for me and provided for me? Or do I fight fear and anger, and discontentment? Do I allow these things to turn me into a grouch? Sometimes, we may simply need an internal perspective reboot to get back to wonder.

Paul David Tripp, in his book "AWE: Why it Matters for Everything we Think, Say, and Do" says that *all sin problem is an awe problem*. When we are not in awe of all God is and all He does, we will live our life selfishly. We will worship creation and forget the Creator. Wonder is the key to living a fulfilled and grateful life. Wonder allows us to discover purpose and a never-ending growth path. The ability to see the blessing in being small and not the center of the universe is the key to finding that purpose. When we are content to be the small fish in the ocean, it is always a better perspective than constantly being seduced to be a big fish in a small pond.

Walking the journey for the journey's sake is the whole point. Arriving "there" will only happen the day we stand before Him and can bow at His feet. Until then, we keep walking, we keep discovering, we go from glory to glory and faith to faith.

Wonder gives us the ability to lean into love and forgiveness, to embrace meekness and mercy, to let go of bitterness and retaliation, to turn the other cheek. It gives us the ability to see the deeper meaning beyond the way things appear. Wonder is what brings us to an eternal perspective that only God can give.

Someone said, "I want to be among the easily impressed." When was the last time your heart skipped a beat because of a discovery that illuminated your heart and mind?

Wonder is the key to worship, looking into the face of Jesus and being transformed.

> *The LORD is in his holy temple,*
> *let all the earth be silent before him.*
> (Habakkuk 2:20) NIV

> *The whole earth is filled with awe at your wonders;*
> *where morning dawns, where evening fades,*
> *you call forth songs of joy.*
> (Psalms 65:8) NIV

Take some time early in the morning to start your day with a perspective challenge. Here is a hymn to start your journey:

Oh Lord, my God, when I in awesome wonder
Consider all the worlds Thy hands have made
I see the stars, I hear the rolling thunder
Thy power throughout the universe displayed

Then sings my soul, my Savior God, to Thee
How great Thou art

Spend the entire day challenging your thoughts to wonder.

HEART QUESTIONS TO PONDER:

How am I blessed?

What has He done for me that is truly "wonder-full"?

Have I thanked God for all that He is and all
He has done and is doing?

2

ARE YOU HARD TO IMPRESS? I JOHNATHAN DEAN

Johnathan is the Worship Pastor at First Church, Pearland, Texas. He is a recording artist and has led (and leads) worship on many national stages. He is passionately pursuing the awe of God.

Are you hard to impress? Well, are you? With everything at our fingertips these days, we are on sensory overload. Technology, social media and all of its filters, Hollywood and so many other things...everything is so polished. So perfect. For creatives and artsy people, this process is inspiring. And we may even seek to recreate what we've seen in our own worship environments.

But I wonder, though, how much has our ability to be "wow'ed" been affected? We see something new or impressive and it never registers how amazing "that something" was because we see amazing things all of the time.

I feel the same may be true in our walk of faith. Our worship. And more specifically, our worship to our King. Have we become accustomed to being in His presence? Is it something we expect and don't anticipate? Does it "wow" us like it should? We feel His presence near and often, but do we take it for granted?

On average, a child asks about 125 questions per day. (Having kids of my own, I not only believe this is true, but question if the number is kinda low – at least some days.) As adults, we have exchanged awe and wonder for apathy and only ask about an average of 6 questions per day. That is 119 less!

Psalm 40:5 (NIV) says,

> *Many, Lord my God, are the wonders you have done,*
> *the things you planned for us.*
> *None can compare with you;*
> *were I to speak and tell of your deeds,*
> *they would be too many to declare.*

And the Message says it like this:

> *The world's a huge stockpile of*
> *God-wonders and God-thoughts.*
> *Nothing and no one comes close to you!*
> *I start talking about you, telling what I know,*
> *and quickly run out of words.*
> *Neither numbers nor words account for you.*

So what are some enemies of wonder? Let's name a few: Hurry. Stress. Too much technology. Lack of solitude. Boredom of routine. Noise of our day-to-day lives. Information overload. Demands. Absence of collaboration. Habits. All of these things (to name a few) fight wonder and creativity.

If I'm being honest, oftentimes I can find myself at the end of a day having made no space for the presence of God. The wonder of it all. Creator of the universe. How can I overlook His care for me and the attention He gives to every detail of my life? Yet time and again I do.

He is Jesus. Savior and King of my life. He is the God who became flesh and chose to pay an ultimate sacrifice so I could have a chance at salvation and abundant life. Yet I get busy while He watches and waits for the smallest acknowledgement of His presence.

I want to be a worship leader whose praise and worship is built on a foundation of gratitude and wonder. I want to be among those that are easily impressed by Him, His creation and His beauty.

I want to find myself growing in capacity for wonder and awe. I want to be awe-filled. I want to be lost in the wonder of who He is.

It's really simple. If we find the wonder of who He is, our worship would be continual. As a matter of fact, when we come face to face with Him, the only response *is* worship. There's no right way or formula to follow. Just worship. The only wrong thing to do is nothing.

Find space in every moment to be more aware of His presence and the wonder of it all...Jesus Christ.

HEART QUESTIONS TO PONDER:

Which wonder-thief is robbing you the most?

Do I struggle with disdain when things don't meet my
standard of perfection?

3

GUARDING OUR LANDMARKS I MATT EWING

Matt is the Minister of Music at Eastwood Pentecostal Church in Lake Charles, LA. He is a proficient musician on multiple instruments and has a unique prophetic anointing in his life. He comes from a powerful Apostolic heritage, but it is his pure heart and love for the Word of God that makes him a treasured friend and voice.

> *Ye are the light of the world.*
> *A city set on a hill cannot be hid.*
> *(Matthew 5:14) ASV*

There is in every man a desire to be accepted. From childhood we are conditioned to seek approval from parents, guardians, or friends. Many studies and tests have proven that we want to fit in, and will do some strange things to accomplish it. We understand from this insight why God would tell his people in Deuteronomy 7 (KJV):

> *When the LORD thy God shall bring thee into the land whither thou goest to possess it...*
> *thou shalt make no covenant with them...*
> *For they will turn away thy son from following me, that they may serve other gods:*
> *...For thou art an holy people unto the LORD thy God: the LORD thy God hath chosen thee to be a special people unto himself, above all people that are upon the face of the earth.*

In this passage, God is warning His people against becoming comfortable with the influence of unbelievers. We all can begin to unknowingly conform to things that are not Christ-like. The "Asch Conformity Experiment" is a clear example of this tendency.

In the 1950s, Dr. Solomon Asch conducted a series of studies called the Conformity Experiment. With each test, he used a number of associates with one test subject, or participant. The associates, prior to the test, would agree to pick an incorrect answer. The participant would then get asked for their answer after all others were given. When the associates intentionally gave a wrong answer, about 75% of participants conformed at least once, while only 25% of participants never conformed.

In a second series of tests, with no pressure of a wrong answer given by his associates, less than 1% of participants gave the wrong answer. Dr Asch's conclusion was people will conform for two main reasons: because they want to fit in with the group, or, because they believe the group is better informed than they are.

Landmarks are described as either a significant event that marks a turning point, or a prominent object whereby one could establish their location. Without a solid understanding of, and a genuine love for our biblical landmarks, we can become like the 75% in Dr. Asch's study. It's far too easy to let pressure sway us away from the truths that we should fiercely cherish.

As a musician, I have had lucrative opportunities that would have required me to lay aside my Godly convictions. By God's grace, I have had family and leaders in my life who walked the path before, and taught me to treasure the old landmarks. Their voices reminded me of why the landmarks existed. I've had friends who were not as fortunate. They followed fame or fortune and most learned, sadly, they could not maintain their spiritual identity and make it back.

It is far too easy to confuse "separate from the world" and "separate from sinners" in an effort to sincerely show the love of Christ. We must be careful that not to lose our landmarks. They make us unique to the world. How will the world find a spiritual landmark in us if we begin to blur the lines? It is ok to be excellent. It is ok to sing before an audience of sinners in an attempt to reach them. However, no matter the situation, we must let the light of God shine unblemished.

The Eiffel Tower was disdained at its start, and almost torn down. It wasn't until years later that the Parisians became fond of it. Sometimes it takes years of living before landmarks are cherished.

My grandfather, the late Reverend Murrell Ewing, frequently said, "Never remove a fence until you know why it was built." In the same sense, don't remove the landmarks and things that make you different in order to fit in with a world that lacks direction. The landmark is serving a purpose.

The landmarks God places in our lives become our anchor. They also become the things that define us in the eyes of others. So, whether we have an offer to sing or play before millions or serve our congregation, let's decide to be less concerned with, "*Does the world accept my sound or my style*?" and more concerned with, "*Are my landmarks identifiable to others*?" Let's retain wonder for the treasured landmarks that define our faith.

HEART QUESTIONS TO PONDER:

Do I struggle with the pressure to conform to the opinions of others? How do I realign my spirit with God's intention for my ministry?

What profound landmarks exist in my life? (A wise voice? A spiritually impacting moment? A biblical principle?)

How do I safeguard these landmarks?

Say a prayer today of thanks for the landmarks in your life. Find fresh wonder in the principles that keep your walk with God centered.

OUR VOICE MATTERS I RAMONA GRIFFITH

Ramona is a pastor's wife and worship leader from Herrin, IL. She is a gifted vocalist who has graced multiple recordings through the years. Her humble spirit and sensitivity to God is a treasure to all who know her.

> *Let the words of my mouth,*
> *and the meditation of my heart, be acceptable in thy sight,*
> *O Lord, my strength, and my redeemer.*
> (Psalm 19:14) KJV

Our Creator listens to many voices. Yet the human voice resonates more clearly with Him than any other. Hebrews 4:15 states that He is "moved" or "touched" (having strong emotion or compassion) with the feelings of our infirmities (KJV). Our voice then, is more important to God than any other noise to be heard. It is imperative that as worship leaders, we recognize how important our single voice is, and how important our combined voices of worship are to God. He is listening to every nuance. He hears what we cannot even say; the voiced and the unvoiced all matter to God.

We must never underestimate the power of our voice… and how it affects not only people, but also the spirit world … and especially God. Our single voice matters so much to God that as He collects our praise, He doesn't just do so as one great chorus, but He hears and notes the individual sound of each voice. He listens to the sounds of heartbreak; He hears the sounds of triumph; He aches with the sound of our despair. And He is moved the most by our love.

My Dad was a man of the Word. He often shared nuggets from the Scriptures and challenged me to check them out for myself. The last time he shared a scriptural truth was shortly before he passed away. He described to me the grandeur of the throne of God in Revelation chapters 4 and 5. He talked about the elders who surround the throne in their white raiment and crowns of gold. He described the sea of glass like crystal and the splendid beasts which gave glory to God continually. He told of the book no one was worthy to open. When John wept about this, one of the elders told him not to weep because the Lion of the Tribe of Judah, the Root of David, was worthy to open the book.

My Dad described all of this in detail. Then he said, "Read chapter 5, verse 6. The ONE who was in the middle of all of that glory, the only ONE worthy to open the book, was *a lamb as it had been slain*." I asked him what it all meant. He said, "Just think about it." That was the end of the conversation and we never discussed it again.

One day, not much later, I was overwhelmed with my life. Situations with relatives and with pastoring a church were weighing me down. I went to the prayer room when no one was at the church, and knelt down and did what Dad instructed me to do... I didn't ask God for strength or share my frustrations. I just focused on the Lamb as it had been slain.

I began to visualize that in the middle of the glory and the majesty of the throne of God, was a gory mess. As my mind and heart began to process the significance of that, and as I recognized the true holiness of God and the beauty of His sacrifice, the Spirit of God transported me into His throne room. It is the only time in my life that I can say I sat directly at His feet.

I have no idea how much time elapsed that day. It could have been moments or hours. I do not know. What I do know is the incredible experience of true worship that erupted out of my silence. There was no "flesh" in that experience. I can't say that I totally understand everything I saw and felt. Yet, my human spirit communed with Eternal God. My human voice affirmed Almighty God. Imagine that. He allowed me to elevate Him. He gave me the gift of worship.

Now, each time I have the privilege to stand before the congregation, as lead worshiper, I am more aware than ever that I stand before the holiness of our Creator. When I lift my voice with many voices, or if I do so alone, He knows MY voice. He knows every shade of my voice. He hears each one of us. And we should never underestimate the power of our voice in the earthly realm, the spirit world, and especially to God Himself.

> *Death and life*
> *are in the power of the tongue..*
> (Proverbs 18:21) ASV

Our voice matters to God.

HEART QUESTIONS TO PONDER:

When you go before God, do you feel your voice has value?

How is God's attentiveness to our voice part of the "wonder" of who He is?

What experiences have made you aware of the holiness of our Creator?

TIMELESS WORSHIP | BISHOP JIMMY SHOEMAKE
Excerpted from "Transference of Apostolic Anointing"
Heart of Worship 2018

Bishop Shoemake has served the Apostolic movement as a profound leader and influencer for many years. Not only did he pastor First Church in San Jose, CA for 25 years, but has served as a trusted leader on the national level. Music has always been close to his heart; he plays the electric and upright bass.

> *But as it is written: 'Eye has not seen, nor ear heard,*
> *nor have entered into the heart of man*
> *the things which God has prepared for those who love Him.'*
> *(1 Corinthians 2:9) KJV*

If you are involved in the praise team or praying for the praise team, I want you to understand praise opens the door for God to manifest Himself in ways that are powerful and miraculous. These powerful manifestations are comforting, educating, strengthening, and life-giving. All of these are possible because in the presence of God we are in the presence of creation!

Praise opens the door for the creative spirit and power of Almighty God to be manifested. If something is missing in our lives, God can create it when we are in His presence.

Luke 17 tells of the 10 lepers that Jesus healed and how one leper returned to thank Jesus. Leprosy causes nerve damage, and with a lack of feeling lepers often lose fingers and other extremities. But one man came back to Jesus and thanked Him for what He had done. Jesus said, "Go your way, you've been made whole." This leads me to believe that if any of the leper's fingers or toes were missing, they were made whole. If a nose had been lost, it was restored. When we are in the presence of God, we are in the presence of creative power and there is no limit to what God can do.

Understanding this can broaden the prospects of effective ministry – whether on your knees in prayer, sitting in the audience praising God in times of corporate worship, or with another worshiper exalting God and allowing God to manifest Himself.

When we have access to technology and equipment, it can be used for the Kingdom of God. We must understand these things have nothing to do with anointing or the power of God. Anointing begins not with a beautiful building, not with the latest of technology, and not with the most comfortable seating. Anointing begins in our relationship with Almighty God and in understanding that He is the source of all that we need.

God is everywhere, but God does not manifest Himself everywhere. However, when our hearts are open, God will manifest Himself in miraculous ways. When we worship God, we are bridging the gap between humanity and divinity. This is why praise and worship is vitally important. It is not important whether the congregation hears the latest musical progressions and sounds. There is nothing wrong with those things. God can use them if they are anointed. It is not important that we sing the latest songs. The songs I want to sing are songs that come from an anointed heart, a passionate heart of love, written by someone who saw God revealed in a beautiful way.

Ephesians 2:6 says *"He has raised us up together, and made us sit together in heavenly places."* How do we reach those heavenly places? There are times in church or at home when we actually move into heavenly places where our sorrows vanish, our aches disappear and our problems are solved in our minds because we aren't worrying about them. There won't be any worries in heaven, and our worries disappear when we are worshiping in those heavenly places.

We can praise with broken hearts because we know the Bible promises us a day is coming when God is going to wipe away all tears from our eyes. The promise is that there will be no more death, no more sorrow nor crying. There shall be no more pain.

> *For the former things are passed away,*
> *And he that sat upon the throne said,*
> *Behold, I make all things new.*
> Revelation 21:4-5 (KJV)

What wonderful opportunities exist when a worship leader or praise team understands that successful praise comes from preparing on our knees before God. I learned a long time ago, if I am going to be effective as a minister, I must prepare that message with prayer. I need to spend time with God, not just offering a little "God bless the service tonight" prayer, but praying until my heart touches God. When I touch God in prayer I can step to the pulpit with assurance, not in my ability, but assurance that if I give my best, God is going to show up and something good is going to happen. I know the source of my anointing. When I invest time in connecting with God, He is able to do anything!

I challenge you to lead congregations into places of timeless worship by entering into heavenly places on your knees. Do not only lead others, but determine to experience a personal session of timeless worship in prayer today.

HEART QUESTIONS TO PONDER:

Am I setting aside enough time in prayer on a regular basis for entering into "heavenly places"?

Do I perceive any lack of resources (equipment, personnel, etc.) as a hindrance to anointing?

THE PURPOSE OF
YOUR GIFT

BRING ME A MINSTREL | JEFFREY HARPOLE
Excerpted from "Bring Me A Minstrel" sermon at Heart of Worship 2019

Rev. Harpole pastors New Life Fellowship in Terre Haute, IN. He is also an anointed singer, saxophonist and recording artist. He is passionate about worship and has nurtured a dynamic worship team in the local church.

So the king of Israel went,
and the king of Judah, and the king of Edom:
and they fetched a compass of seven days' journey:
and there was no water for the host, and for the cattle that followed them.
(2 Kings 3:9) KJV

Marcus Garvey once wrote *"A people without knowledge of their past, origin, or culture is like a tree without roots."* History is the teacher of all things, an arrow which guides us from one place to another. To know where we are, we must know from where we have come. Let's consider this Biblical account that specifically involved a musician.

2 Kings tells us the story of Jehoram, son of Ahab who comes to power as King over a people that are fractured and divided. The united kingdom of David has faded. Jehorman himself is a mixed bag. History will show he rejects some of the needless bloodshed of his father. He has some interest in the true worship of his predecessors, but walks divided, continuing to promote false gods. Somehow, he has made peace with the righteous king of Judah, and together they set out to defeat a common enemy.

These kings march their armies for seven days and then disaster strikes. They find themselves without direction, food, or water. Their strength had run out. And like so many of us so much of the time, it wasn't until complete depletion that someone asked God for help.

Jehoshaphat, the King traveling with Jehoram, knows they made a mistake, and instead of blaming God he asked the pivotal question: "Is there not a prophet of the Lord we can inquire?" The answer comes from one of the officers of Jehoram. He says, "Yes. The prophet's name is name is Elisha."

Elisha, the powerful prophet, steps forward into this uncomfortable scene. Three kings are appealing for his advice. Remember, this is Elisha who has witnessed numerous miracles, including seeing an axe head float. He is anointed. He is gifted. He shouldn't need anything else or anyone to speak the Word of the Lord. However, *this* environment is filled with flesh and the prophet can sense it. The prophet knows he cannot deliver a word in this atmosphere. So he says something profound. He makes a simple request: "Bring me a minstrel." I need a musician. I need a worshiper.

The prophet, the bearer of the Word of God, needed a musician to carry a spirit of worship into the atmosphere. This is a powerful principle that lasts today. Anointed musicianship is needed to bring order in the spirit world when there is an atmosphere of confusion. The minstrel declares order to the swirling thoughts of those who are not in tune. Before the Word is brought forth, there needs to be a musician capable of giving order to the chaos.

Have you ever looked at the life of Elvis Presley. The rock star adored by millions grew up singing the hymns of the church. So it was, even when he captured large crowds and adoring fans there was emptiness. This void drew him back to the songs of his mother.

At the height of his fame, also present in his life were soaring addictions. However, it was the songs of the Lord that calmed his life. Close friends and band members commented on the peace that would fall in private moments when Elvis would sing songs like 'He Touched Me'. A conflicted and addicted super star found order and peace in worship.

Our churches need anointed minstrels. The chaos of the world demands someone who can restore order using their God-given gifting. The church needs musicians who not only play or sing well, but understand how to break down spiritual barriers and pave the way for the Word.

If you have ever felt insignificant in your gifting, consider that Elisha could not move forward in his ministry without the powerful ministry of a minstrel. Minstrels till the field of the heart, so that it is soft and ready for the Word. When you sense the swirling mess of confusion, pain, and conflict in the people around you and in the world, recognize that God appointed YOUR song to bring peace.

HEART QUESTIONS TO PONDER:

As a worshiper, have I considered my relationship to the prophets in my life, and the importance of my music in the delivery of God's Word?

How does music speak peace over troubled situations and troubled minds?

"Minstrels till the field of the heart, so that it is soft and ready for the Word." How does your ministry help to till the heart?

THE BEAUTY OF o-BE-dience | EMILEE HUDSPETH

Emilee is the famous "girl drummer" from The Pentecostals of Alexandria, LA. Beyond her remarkable musicianship, she has a heart for God and for mentoring people.

He will fulfill the desire of those who fear and worship Him [with awe-inspired reverence and obedience]; He also will hear their cry and will save them.
(Psalms 145:19) AMP

Beautiful friends,

Do you ever wish there was something about yourself you could change? Do you wish you had more confidence? Could trust easily? Could love without limits? Do you wish you could change the sound of your laugh? The color of your eyes? Maybe your height?

There's someone I want you to meet. His name is Zacchaeus.

I'm sure most of you are familiar with the song we learned growing up in Sunday School that describes him as " ..a wee little man.." God knew Zacchaeus was short, because that's exactly how he made him. He wasn't the most popular or loyal guy. Actually, the Bible says he was a well-known sinner. Yet Zacchaeus had no idea this particular day, that Jesus would be visiting him and his home. There was no event on Facebook where Jesus could check in and select "interested" or "going." No "Save the Date" card was sent out. Zacchaeus had no idea Jesus was on His way.

I'm sure he had heard of this man named Jesus. Jesus was popular! Crowds were following Him following everywhere. I'm sure Zacchaeus wondered, "How can I get to him? People are basically stepping on top of me! People are pushing and shoving. How will I ever be able to see Jesus?! He definitely won't be able to see me."

Zacchaeus then sees the sycamore tree. The Bible says he ran ahead of the crowd to climb it. Sometimes, we have to separate ourselves from the crowd to see Jesus clearly with no distractions.

Upon researching sycamore trees, I learned they are actually massive trees! Described as grand and majestic, they average 60 to 100 feet tall having large trunks and bulky seed clusters all over. If it was fully grown and covered with leaves, I'm sure Zacchaeus was hard to spot... but not for Jesus.

> *When Jesus reached the place,*
> *He looked up and said to him,*
> *'Zacchaeus, hurry and come down,*
> *for today I must stay at your house.'*
> (Luke 19:5) AMP

Jesus, did you say today? The house is nowhere near ready for company! And Jesus, did you say STAY at my house?! I didn't make the bed this morning, let alone wash the sheets! The dishes are piled. I'll have to go get groceries. What should I cook?!

Once reality sank in, Zacchaeus probably began thinking, "*Why me, Jesus?! I'm so unqualified. I'm dishonest. I'm short.*" But Jesus already knew all of that. And He even knew his house might be a complete mess. Sort of like his life.

Interestingly, nowhere in this passage do I find where it says that Zacchaeus and his spouse took Jesus to their home. You don't have to be married to have meaning in the kingdom. And you're never too small, too young, or too old either. By simply *being* who God created Him to be, short stature and all, Zacchaeus was given the opportunity to serve this greatest guest of all in his very own home.

The Bible says he hurried down, welcoming Jesus with joy. When the people saw this, they began muttering in discontent. Sometimes when you're obedient to God it will cause people to fuss. People can make you start second guessing yourself, just like the enemy.

> *Did Jesus really say that?*
> *Did He really mean to say that*
> *He wants to visit me in my house?"*

But the words of God will always triumph over what people say. Stay close to Him, so you'll always be able to recognize His voice. There is favor in obedience! And because Zacchaeus was obedient, Jesus said to Him:

> *Salvation has come to this home today…*
> *for the Son of Man came*
> *to seek and save those who are lost.*
> (Luke 19:9-10) NLT

You may feel lost today. You may feel burned out. You may feel tired of the journey. You may even feel like a complete mess. But Jesus knew you'd be here today. So today, I simply ask you to just "BE". Be in each moment. Be in His presence. Be obedient to His word and His house. Be fulfilled in Him and the gifting's He has given you. Just be YOU. Because that's the most beautiful person you can be, and that is exactly who He is looking for.

HEART QUESTIONS TO PONDER:

Am I intentionally making time to "hear" His voice?
What is He speaking to me?

What distractions keep me from being close to God?

Do I struggle to genuinely accept the person
God formed me to be?

GOD'S PLAN FOR THE CREATIVE I
SAVANNAH SULLIVAN

Savannah Sullivan is a creative young leader from Goodlettsville, TN. She is a graphic artist, a photographer and a dynamic worship leader who loves to see art of all kinds elevated in church ministry.

> *Come, all of you who are gifted craftsmen.*
> *Construct everything that the Lord has commanded:*
> (Exodus 35:10) NLT

If you're like me, you've always felt a little different from other people. You think different, you feel different, you just *are* different. Sometimes it's hard to describe, and most times it's hard to relate to others who don't have that same spark you do: The spark of the creative mind.

I'm *not* saying we're more special, because every personality type is needed in God's kingdom, but I *am* saying that indescribable ache swirling around in your heart was placed there for a special purpose.

Exodus chapters 35 and 36 share the account of the construction of the first Tabernacle, the Ark of the Covenant, and all of the tabernacle furnishings. It starts with a call to the nation of Israel to bring their possessions and abilities to build the tabernacle together as a community. Heading up the project is a man named Bezalel, of the tribe of Judah.

Man might be a loose term by today's standards, because according to rabbinical tradition, Bezalel was believed to have been younger than 18 years old. Yet, it was this young man whom God entrusted to carry out His divine plan.

Moses recounts this time in Exodus 35:30-33, saying that God had specifically chosen Bezalel, filled him with His spirit, giving him great wisdom, ability, and expertise in all kinds of crafts. It goes on to list an extraordinary amount of creative talents with which God blessed this young person.

Joining Bezalel is Oholiab, of the tribe of Dan. Together, Moses tells us that God has not only given these two men these amazing talents, but also the ability to teach their craft to others and lead their team to the completion of the Tabernacle.

This passage is chock full of wonderful principles, so let's touch on just a few of them.

When God has a plan, He will speak it through spiritual authorities. Moses heard specifically from God regarding the plan for the tabernacle. Every step of the way, Moses encouraged the community of Israel to help with the project. He endorsed Bezalel, Oholiab, and their team. Moses assisted in any way that he could.

The anointing placed on you by your spiritual leaders is paramount to the success of your calling. It reveals that you have received approval from God, and it reveals to the community that they should approve of your calling as well. (Ex 35:29-30,36:2,3)

When God has a plan, He will send help. Bezalel and Oholiab couldn't build this tabernacle with just the two of them. You can have all the talent and expertise in the world, yet you will always need people to help you execute the plan. Just as God gave you the talents, he will give you the ability to teach your skills because 1) You're not a one-man show, you're going to *need* help, and 2) God doesn't want your talents to die with you. Legacy matters to the kingdom of God. (Ex 36:1-2)

You're also going to need practical resources like materials, funds, and other blessings of the people around you. This is where other personality types play a huge role in your creative endeavors. The Bible says the people who provided resources for the team of creatives were both men and women whose hearts were stirred, whose spirits were moved, and whose hearts were willing. None of those qualities require an ounce of creativity! (Ex 35:21-22a)

When God has a plan, He will equip you with the abilities you need. God gave this team of people remarkable talents to accomplish His plan. In His infinite wisdom, God knew that one day each person would need the specific skills to accomplish the task at hand. Think on this: He sets in motion, from your conception to your death, the path of growth you need to accomplish any given task at the appointed time. He knows what you're going to need to know before you even know that you need to know it! (Ex 35:31-35)

There was a need, and God granted each person the *wisdom and*

ability to perform any task involved in building the sanctuary.
(Exodus 36:1) NLT

When God has a plan, He will give you more than you need. When
the workers set to building the tabernacle, the community
continued to bring in materials. They brought in so much that the
workers had to ask the community to *stop giving.* (Exodus 36:3-7)
When God sets a plan in motion, He knows how much we're going
to need. He will do it... *Exceeding, abundantly, above all that we
can ask or think.* (Ephesians 3:20) KJV

When God has a plan, He will finish it. This amazing feat of talent
and skill was accomplished in approximately 7 months. Together,
the nation of Israel constructed the place where God's people
would come to give, to sacrifice, to make atonement, to give
thanks, and to worship… that place of connection, and *yet...*
separation. That place which mirrors the temple of our hearts, was
entrusted to be built by the hearts and minds of the creative.

Here is God's plan for you. Construct the place in which He would
be pleased to dwell. First, start in your *own* heart, and then allow it
to burst forth, overflowing to the physical and spiritual
environments around you.

Today, feel the weight of the gifts God has given you, and use
them for His divine purpose.

HEART QUESTIONS TO PONDER:

With whom am I sharing my abilities and experience?

What can I do today to begin passing on the baton to the next generation?

What is God asking me to accomplish with my gifts?

What's holding me back?

YOU, YES YOU, ARE VALUABLE I DARLENE BOYT

Darlene has served as a worship pastor, worship leader, clinician, speaker and mentor for over 40 years. Her passion is mentoring the younger generation and helping them discover their hidden talents.

For we are God's handiwork,
created in Christ Jesus to do good works,
which God prepared in advance for us to do.
(Ephesians 2:10) NIV

For you created my inmost being;
you knit me together in my mother's womb.
I praise you because I am fearfully and wonderfully made; your works
are wonderful, I know that full well.
(Psalm 139:13-14) NIV

Fear ye not therefore,
ye are of more value than many sparrows.
(Matthew 10:31) KJV

What comes to mind when you think of the word valuable? Perhaps important. Perhaps something you treasure.

When was the last time you thought about how important you are to God? That He considers YOU a Masterpiece? That you're His treasure?

Or, do you receive your value from the many personality tests? Are you proud to declare yourself a lion, an activator, a competitor, ENFP or a High D? While personality tests can, at times, bring helpful insight...do you have as much desire to know what God thinks about you? Who does God say you are?

Be reminded today that you, yes YOU are valuable. So valuable to God - the God of the Universe -that He came to this earth so we would be restored unto HIM! I am God's handiwork. He made ME!

Often times we compare our value to:

What others think of us.
How successful we are in our education or careers.
How much money is in our bank account.
How many followers we have on social media.
How many likes we get on a post.

None of these determine our value. My value is determined by WHO made me! That is more important than any number of likes or number of followers. It is more important than our financial worth or career success. Our value is only attainable through Jesus Christ! Today's culture focuses on beauty, intelligence, wealth or perhaps talents. God's view of us is internal... not external.

Hollywood has created unrealistic expectations and we have bought into them, creating frustration and a negative self-image.

Relationships affect how we deem our self-worth and value. I have not always viewed myself as valuable. Even though I've spoken those words to many, I struggled with seeing myself as valuable to God and others. It was a constant battle between what I read in God's Word and what I felt.

One day I came to a stark realization that certain relationships were affecting my self-worth and how I viewed myself. How would you view your relationship with the people closest to you? With the people you allow to speak into your life? Do they build you up or tear you down? We have one life to live...I want my life to be surrounded by people that are confirming my worth and not tearing me down.

Relationships on social media have caused all of us to compare ourselves with one another. Our inner dialogue can sound like this:

"Their house is larger than mine...they obviously have more money than I to do...her skin is flawless...they ALWAYS have a blow out service...their children are perfect...that band NEVER makes a mistake...I will never look as good as they do...their marriage seems without conflict..." and on and on.

We've become so accustomed to viewing social media as reality that we have become numb to our constant comparison of ourselves to others. In the end, we place very little value on ourselves.

As we begin to understand and accept our value in God, we will begin to value others. We will begin to build others up. We will be encouragers.

The enemy knows if he can get us to believe that we have little-to-no value he will ultimately win. This is one of the greatest lies of the enemy. On the flip side, when we DO begin to believe in ourselves, have self-worth and value, we will be productive in every area of our life!

When we place our identity and self-worth in the hands of imperfect people, we set ourselves up to be confused and shaken. God's perfect plan is for us to put our identity and self-worth in Him! We are FEARFULLY and WONDERFULLY made!

No matter what has happened in your life, you will NEVER lose value in God's eyes. We are still priceless...dirty or clean, crumpled or perfectly creased, broken in a million pieces or completely whole. God created you as HIS masterpiece!

I commit to speaking these words of affirmation over myself:

I am a child of God.
I am who HE says I am.
I am valuable.

HEART QUESTIONS TO PONDER:

Do I place more value on what others think or say of me than what Jesus does?

Have I truly accepted the fact that I am valuable just as I am?

CONFRONTING INSECURITIES I KEVIN PAYNE

*Kevin Payne is a licensed Marriage and Family Therapist, pursuing his
doctorate. He is also a licensed Minister with the UPCI, and an instructor
at Urshan College. He is passionate about promoting a healthy church
ministry culture and seeing people overcome dysfunction.*

> *My grace is all you need. My power works best in weakness.
> So now I am glad to boast about my weaknesses,
> so that the power of Christ can work through me.
> That's why I take pleasure in my weaknesses, and in the insults,
> hardships, persecutions, and troubles that I suffer for Christ.
> For when I am weak, then I am strong.*
> II Corinthians 12:9 (NLT)

Nobody likes to confront weakness. Human nature much prefers to
protect itself. It is much easier to put on a façade and pretend as if
everything is ok. It's less easy to admit your own lack of abilities or
lack of skill.

Yet leadership positions and platform ministry often asks us to step
outside of ourselves and move away from our comfort zones. If
you're going to do something for God, you'll probably have to take
a risk. You'll have to risk by doing or saying something that will be
scrutinized by others. Musicians may have to play a song that
challenges their skill level. Singers may be asked to lead in an
environment that is uncomfortable or sing a song that feels like a
stretch. And bam! In that moment, insecurity rears its ugly head.

Miriam Webster defines insecurity as, "1) Not confident or sure (uncertain.) 2) Not adequately guarded or sustained (unsafe.) 3) Not firmly fastened or fixed (shaky.) 4) Not highly stable or well-adjusted. 5) Beset with fear and anxiety.

There are four words that jump out to me from this definition. Uncertain. Unsafe. Shaky. Anxious. Does ministry make you feel this way sometimes? You're not alone. Most worshipers have to address the insecurity that threatens to squelch the gift that God confidently placed inside of them!

Many people who are insecure just don't feel worthy of God's gifting. We put a lot of pressure on ourselves to be perfect or always succeed. That's why we feel shaky or anxious. A part of us knows we're probably going to mess up at some point. But the truth is that people often learn more from failures than they do from successes.

When people share their testimony, they often recount that the most treasured experiences of their life have risen out of a broken moment. Great things can emerge from the things you feel the most insecure about. In fact, God loves to be in fellowship with broken people. So the next time you feel really insecure about who you are, just remember this: brokenness positions you to experience God's grace in unimaginable ways.

See, God isn't asking you to be confident in yourself. He's asking you to be confident in His purpose and calling. Insecurity can serve a beautiful role in our lives: it allows us to lay aside our pride and get comfortable with the "broken and repentant heart" that God desires. (Psalm 51:17) NLT

I'm not a musician or singer. But I am a worshiper. And I can tell instinctively when a worship leader is confident or insecure. I can sense when they are lost in their own worry and anxiety, instead of pointing me to the God of their gift. You may feel shaky or uncertain in your own flesh. But when God opens a door for you to lead or minister to someone else, it's time to recognize that God is inviting you to lay aside thoughts of your own "achievement" or "performance" and point others to the God of broken things. Your value is not in who you are as a singer or musician. Your value is in Christ and the redeeming work of the cross.

It's not God's plan that we only have successes and mountain top experiences. In fact, our self-esteem must accommodate both our success and our failure. We must embrace our insecurities and allow it to be part of the path of discipline in the life of a worshiper.

HEART QUESTIONS TO PONDER:

What is an experience that you thought was a failure that God has used as a testimony in your life?

Think about the things you are insecure about.
Is there any root of pride in this emotion?

11

GIFTING: A CALL TO GROW | NANCI HOLSTON

Nanci is part of the Heart of Worship steering team and has invested almost 30 years of life into the music ministry. She has served as a music pastor, a worship leader for district conferences, and a musical mentor to many. Her insight and spirit-led perspectives are a valuable contribution to God's Kingdom.

> *The servant to whom he had entrusted the five bags of silver came forward with five more and said, 'Master, you gave me five bags of silver to invest, and I have earned five more. The master was full of praise. 'Well done, my good and faithful servant. You have been faithful in handling this small amount, so now I will give you many more responsibilities. Let's celebrate together!' (Matthew 25:20-21) NLT*

Let's take a moment to reflect on how we felt as children, anticipating Christmas or a birthday, any time we hoped to receive a gift. If you were like me, you could hardly contain your excitement! My imagination ran wild, making plans for whatever was hidden under wrapping paper. I was convinced that the new sneakers would guarantee that I would run faster and jump higher, and that the Slinky toy would really 'walk' down the stairs just like the commercial depicted (fail!!!!). Perhaps some of us are still like that; we can hardly contain our joy at the prospect of receiving gifts.

James 4:2 tells us that we often do not have or obtain what we want because we do not ask. Verse 3 further explains that we do not receive what we ask for because we are asking for the wrong thing. Is it possible that we are asking for 'gifts' we do not need, and are blindly looking past the gifts that have already been given to us? It is all too easy for us to downgrade how we perceive our talents because, in our estimation, the talent does not measure up to those we see in others. Perhaps it is time for us to ask the Holy Spirit to illuminate our understanding, and for us to accept responsibility for developing talents that have been generously given by our Maker.

It is not unusual for creatives to doubt the authenticity and God-purpose of their gifting. When viewed through the microscope of self-criticism, weaknesses are magnified. One of the most common struggles for creatives is accepting that God-given abilities are placed in us for Kingdom purposes.

Our gifts are a God-investment. Matthew 25:14-28 demonstrates clearly that God expects a return on His investment. Creative abilities are placed in us for more than personal gratification or entertainment of the masses. Instead, they are tremendously valuable and have the potential to multiply into a powerful source of beauty and blessing. God gives us talent and aptitude with the expectation that we will commit to growing the gifts that were placed in us before we were even born. (Jeremiah 1:5; Galatians 1:15; Psalm 71:6; Psalm 139:13-16)

It is tempting to view ultra-talented individuals as superior. We assume they have been blessed with gifts that are a higher quality than our own. The reality is, without exception, those artists have dedicated thousands of hours to developing their gift, and *this* is what makes their outstanding performances seem effortless. They have responded to the call to grow by investing time and resources in developing their talents.

What if the talent given to the ungrateful servant (Matthew 25) contained more potential than all the talents distributed to the other servants? Did the discouragement of comparison cause him to leave a magnificent source of blessing undeveloped? Could it be that a talent we perceive as "less" is exactly the gift God plans to use as a powerful channel of blessing for others?

Gifting cannot be separated from the challenge to grow. If we are gifted, we are called. If we are called, we are commissioned. The commission carries with it a command and the promise of being equipped. We can move forward by embracing the privilege of being called, commanded, commissioned and equipped to fulfill our Kingdom purpose.

Here are some challenges for creatives:

Develop spiritual strength and godly character. Gifting without spiritual understanding and godly character cannot bring eternal value to the local church or Kingdom of God.

Value our time. Recognize the invaluable resource of time and invest it wisely so that the creative contribution becomes a continual offering of excellence.

Establish emotional maturity. Emotional maturity allows us to aspire to become like creatives we admire without becoming the victims of comparison.

Foster sincere humility. Humility is not devaluing what God has given to us. A humble attitude acknowledges talent and provides protection from the destructive effects of egotism.

Overcome the fear of failure. Fear paralyzes minds, hinders anointing, blocks creative flow, and causes creatives to devalue and bury valuable gifts.

Let's ask God to give us revelation and understanding regarding overlooked potential in the gifts He has already placed in us.

HEART QUESTIONS TO PONDER:

Do I struggle with validating my talent(s) as a gift from God?

What can I do today to grow or refresh the talent(s)
that have been placed in me?

What potential gifts reside in me for which I need to pray for
revelation and understanding?

DISCIPLINES OF THE
WORSHIPER

12

HOW MUCH DO YOU WEIGH? | BETHANY EASTER

Bethany is the music minister at TurningPoint in Madison, TN. She is a gifted worship leader and vocal coach. In addition to serving her local church she has traveled the country as a guest soloist and vocal director for various musical events.

> *Wherefore seeing we also are compassed about*
> *with so great a cloud of witnesses,*
> *let us lay aside every weight,*
> *and the sin which doth so easily beset us,*
> *and let us run with patience the race that is set before us...*
> (Hebrews 12:1) KJV

There is one question in particular that I will only allow my doctor to ask me. Yes, as you have correctly guessed from the title, it has to do with my weight. Some go to great lengths to maintain, change, or conceal their weight. I'm guilty of the latter. Your weight has the potential to affect your overall quality of life. It can hinder where you can and cannot go as well as what you can and cannot do. It determines a lot. As with most cases, the spiritual equivalent to anything physical carries with it a much heavier weight. *Pun intended.*

The writer of Hebrews tells us that there are two separate things we need to put off from us: weights and sin. We all know what blatant sin looks like. However, I want to focus on the first part of the passage.

What is a weight? Well, it's not a sin per se. We know that they are not one and the same because the distinction is made using the word "and" when mentioning both topics. A weight can be anything that is not sinful, but if consumed without moderation, can slowly start to resemble idolatry.

You would be hard pressed to find someone who thought sewing was evil. Considering the little I know about the hobby, I would say it is one of the most tranquil and docile hobbies one could take up. Depending on skill set and ambition, sewing may become time consuming. So, when does the innocent and docile hobby of sewing become a weight? When it loses its proper place and starts to take up your prayer time.

Social media, in and of itself, is not a sin. Many churches have utilized it as a form of outreach and there are many pages dedicated to Christian living, So, when does it become a weight? Well, it does so when we habitually miss opportunities to witness because we're more concerned with scrolling than being sensitive to the people God intentionally allows to cross our path. Enjoying a good book is safe, right? If we neglect our Bible reading to catch up with a personal self-help book, it no longer remains benign.

We must be careful not to let the things that start off as harmless turn into weights that consume our time and energy. If a marathoner ran an important race with weights around their ankles, arms, and neck, they wouldn't be taken seriously. They would be doing themselves a disservice and ultimately cause bodily harm. So why is it that so many of us find ourselves running the most critical race of our lives with unnecessary weights? Many think the only goal is to simply cross the finish line. Yes, that indeed is paramount and imperative. But if our choice is between crossing the finish line weary, due to self-inflicted interference, or crossing the finish line with light abandon, we would choose the latter.

If I can be transparent for a moment, YouTube has been a huge weight for me. From countless cooking tutorials to hair care tips, YouTube has it all. I can follow my favorite podcast with fresh content daily as well as subscribe to various music channels. And since television is basically obsolete due to streaming, I found myself easily watching hours (yes, you read that right…HOURS) of various content. YouTube became the place I received my news, my updates on social and political climate, and where I found new worship music.

Admittedly, I began to feel conviction on how much time ultimately had been surrendered to this pastime. My prayer life was affected and therefore my sensitivity to things of the spirit became dull. I knew the Lord wasn't satisfied with my schedule and He would drop little things in my spirit. Sometimes it would be easy to push that feeling aside. "I'll pray after this video clip," I thought. But that clip turned into seven other clips.

Tolerating my weight would be me trying to fit my prayer life around my unchecked YouTube consumption. Getting rid of my weight would be prioritizing my prayer time and then finding a limited amount of time for YouTube.

Jesus wants our attention. You know it when you feel it, that gentle tugging at your heart. The very One who is responsible for every star in space and keeps the earth spinning at just the right angle is interested in spending time with us. Don't ignore His gentle tugging. Identify what your specific weights are and ask Jesus to help you not to just manage your weight, but to lay it aside.

HEART QUESTIONS TO PONDER:

How much do I spiritually weigh
and what are my weight loss options?

What significant "weight" do I need to work to "set aside?"

Am I truly ready to make my load lighter?
Beware: It's not a diet, it's a lifestyle.

13

POWER IN SURRENDER | JAMES ROBERTS

James is the Minister of Music at Family Worship Center, American Canyon, California. He is a prolific songwriter, worship leader, preacher, and a highly valued Heart of Worship staff Administrator.

"Submit yourselves therefore to God. Resist the devil, and he will flee from you."
(James 4:7) KJV

"Therefore humble yourselves under the mighty hand of God, that He may exalt you in due time, casting all your care upon Him, for He cares for you."
(1 Peter 5:6-7) NKJV

Several years ago, I co-wrote a song called "Learning to Let Go". The bridge says:

"I'm letting go of pride, letting go of fear
Letting go of pain and nights filled with tears
I'm letting go of the lies that have torn me up inside ... "

Many times we hold on to the mistakes we make. Some mistakes are reactions to hurts that come our way. Other mistakes are things we did to ourselves.

Years ago, I was deeply hurt by leadership; someone lied, the lie was believed, and I was shipped out of my home church to "take a ministry opportunity I couldn't pass up," which really meant "go sit down in another church and let God fix you." After three months of doing everything I was asked to do, I was allowed to return to my home church. Things didn't feel right, sound right, or look right.

So, for three months I "obeyed" on the outside. But on the inside, I was churning with anger, bitterness, and resentment. How could an all-knowing God allow this to happen to me? Why did I have to jump through these hoops? Why didn't I get a chance to defend myself? After three months of doing everything I was asked to do, I was allowed to return to my home church. Things didn't feel right, sound right, or look right. In that frame of mind, wearing my hurt-colored glasses, I made the decision to walk away from God and the church.

To make a long story short, I was a prodigal for five years. My current pastor reached out to me time and again, refusing to let my rejection discourage him. He and my entire church family chose to be like Christ and showed love that would not give up.

Fast forward a few more years, and now I was the music minister at my church and involved in Singles Ministry for the district. Everything looked great on the outside, but inside I was still dealing with hurts that I didn't really want to carry. But I wouldn't leave my own weights behind because they justified my victim mentality and bitterness. At a District Singles Conference I was leading worship and singing my song "Learning to Let Go." The speaker told a personal story about writing their hurts on rocks, praying over them, and letting the ocean carry them away as a sign of surrender. In this way, he signified to God that he would not hold on to hurt any longer.

I took this to heart. I was really tired of carrying around the weight of bitterness. Two friends and I went to the Pacific Ocean with sharpies in hand. We wrote down every hurt and the person's name who inflicted the pain on the rocks. We prayed over them, and like 1 Peter 5:7 says, we "cast our cares on Him" by casting the rocks into the ocean. We said, "God, we're done! These weights now belong to You; we don't want to carry these ever again."

I know beyond a shadow of a doubt God heard that prayer. The very next day, as I was sitting in a restaurant, I saw one of the people whose name I had written on a rock less than 24 hours earlier. Before that day, I had not seen my offender for ten years! Knowing the hurt that I had carried for that long decade, I considered leaving before the food arrived. However, I was completely fine.I refused to be bothered by something I couldn't change. I chose to live looking up to the Healer of Hurts, instead of focusing on those who had hurt me.

Surrender means to give up, to hand over authority, simply to submit or yield.

Is there any other being with more power than Jesus Christ? If we really believe that Jesus spoke the entire universe into existence, are we going to stubbornly insist that our issues are too big, too hard, or too insurmountable for Him to eradicate?

Honestly, sometimes it's hard to break out of our own flawed thinking. We aren't sure that God will handle our issues, so we keep holding on to hurts, reliving them day after day, year after year, selling ourselves short of the greatness God sees in us. But when we "lay aside every weight, and the sin which so easily ensnares us," like Hebrews 12 states, then we can truly experience the healing power of surrender.

I challenge you today to write down the things you are tired of carrying. Do something with that list that shows God you are choosing the power of surrender. Tear up the list. Throw it in the fireplace. Release it in a balloon. Or give it to a trusted friend. Do something today that shows you are laying down your weights and that you are determined today not to pick them up again.

HEART QUESTIONS TO PONDER:

What fear, lie, or pain am I holding on to?

Are these things keeping me from stepping into the season that God has planned for me?

14

PURITY I REV. JOE ZIRPOLI

Joe is a full time evangelist and licensed minister with the United Pentecostal Church, as well as a gifted songwriter, recording artist and worship leader. His love for truth is evident as he shares the Word of God everywhere he goes.

> *Take away the dross from the silver,*
> *and there shall come forth a vessel for the finer.*
> (Proverbs 25:4) KJV

What is purity? Purity is what is left over after sins and weights are removed from our lives.

Dross is the waste material that is discarded through the process of refining silver. To obtain pure silver, dross (impurities) must be removed. Not all impurities are removed at one time, but after some dross is extracted, the silversmith turns up the heat in order to extract more. The same process goes for us. Becoming pure is continuous. The Psalmist's prayer request should also be ours.

> *Search me, O God,*
> *and know my heart: try me, and know my thoughts:*
> *And see if there be any wicked way in me,*
> *and lead me in the way everlasting.*
> (Psalm 139:23-24) KJV

In college, I took a public speaking course. I was taught the importance of cutting out "filler" words, habitual gestures, and countless other small distractions which take away from the presentation.

Recently, I watched a video of myself preaching. I was mortified by the amount of times I said the word, "Amen" in my sermon. Saying "Amen" every other word had not always been a practice in my preaching, but somewhere along the way, I picked up this unhealthy habit. Additionally, I noted three specific distractions in appearance, words, and actions. I vowed to correct them immediately.

In our walk with God, we can pick up impurities along the way and not even realize it. These impurities distract from our presentation.

If any man be in Christ,
he is a new creature: old things are passed away;
behold, all things are become new.
(2 Corinthians 5:17) KJV

When the apostle Paul speaks these words, his verbiage is present tense. The newness is ongoing. Christ's plan is to continually make us more like Him. He not only sees our potential, but requires us to fulfill it. (1Peter 1:15-16)

If we do not strive to keep things new in our relationship with Christ, the clear channel between God and us becomes clogged with impurities. Then the channel between His people and us will also be affected. His power and authority cannot effectively flow and make any significant difference in the lives of others.

We live in a sinful world. Although we do not need to live in fear of falling into temptation, we need to avoid carelessly taking on impurities. (Galatians 5:13) KJV

At times, the cares of life can weigh us down. We have seemingly endless responsibilities, and not enough time to fulfill them. The natural tendency of carnality is to entertain evil desires and distractions. (Romans 7:19) Sins and/or weights, along with a carnal man's willingness to indulge them, are a recipe for impurity. The writer of Hebrews commands us to:

> *...lay aside every weight and the sin*
> *which doth so easily beset us...*
> (Hebrews 12:1) KJV

How do we accomplish this? A good practice is to train yourself to ask, "*Is this thought, word, or action I am about to entertain consecration to God, or a channel for impurity?*"

How do we remain sensitive enough to know the difference? We must stoke the fire of the Holy Spirit daily! Praying in the spirit will consistently purify us. The hotter the fire, the more impurities, inconsistent with His holiness, will be extracted from our lives.

> *Blessed are the pure in heart:*
> *for they shall see God.*
> (Matthew 5:8) KJV

The choices we make to pursue purity not only allow us to show God to others, but they allow us to see and encounter the glory of God in own lives. Let us all be committed to continually shaking off weights and walking forward with newness in Christ.

HEART QUESTIONS TO PONDER:

Are my thoughts, words, or actions moving me closer to God or creating a channel for impurity?

How do I nurture my own spiritual sensitivity towards things that may negatively impact my purity?

Do I have any habits that have become distractions in my witness to others?

TRUE WORSHIP | PARRIS BOWENS

Parris is an amazing artist, musician, leader and deep thinker. He has played on the highest stages of the gospel music industry but is a man of sincere humility who loves God and is devoted to his family.

> *Jesus replied, "Believe me, dear woman, the time is coming when it will no longer matter whether you worship the Father on this mountain or in Jerusalem.*
> *You Samaritans know very little about the one you worship. while we Jews know all about him, for salvation comes through the Jews.*
> *But the time is coming —indeed it's here now— when true worshipers will worship the Father in spirit and in truth. The Father is looking for those who will worship him that way. For God is Spirit, so those who worship him must worship in spirit and in truth."*
> *(John 4:21-24) NLT*

For a number of years, I've toured and played on all kinds of stages all over the world. There's nothing like having a live worship experience with your brothers and sisters in Christ. When I come off the stage people will come up to me from time to time and compliment my playing. I have to admit, that feels good.

But after a long trip or tour I get to my front door, insert the key and turn the lock. Before I can get the door could open, I hear the excited noise of my kids on the other side running to tackle me. "Daddy!!!" They yell as they jump in my arms. One day it hit me. No matter how many people praise me at the engagement, nothing matches the sound of my children's voices welcoming me home.

In the gospel of John chapter 4 verse 23, Jesus says to the Samaritan woman, *"But the time is coming-indeed it's here now-when the true worshipers will worship the Father in spirit and in truth. The Father is looking for those who will worship him that way."*

We know God by many names and attributes, yet it's interesting that when it comes to the topic of worship, Jesus referred to God as the Father. At times we can see worship as a duty or as something in which we are unworthy to participate. It may even seem like a religious practice or ritual. However, if we hear the spirit speaking in this scripture, our Heavenly Father is not looking for any of those types of worshipers. God is looking for his children.

> *About that time the disciples came to Jesus and asked,*
> *"Who is greatest in the Kingdom of Heaven?"*
> *Jesus called a little child to him and put the child among them.*
> *Then he said, "I tell you the truth, unless you turn from your sins*
> *and become like little children, you will never get into the*
> *Kingdom of Heaven. So anyone who becomes as humble*
> *as this little child is the greatest in the Kingdom of Heaven."*
> (Matthew 18:1-4) NLT

Worship is linked to that relationship between a father and his child. While we all appreciate the praise of someone else, it's nothing like the adoration of a child. The loving welcome of my children gives me joy. And that joy in turn gives me strength. So, I imagine that God is equally excited when He hears us worshiping Him, not as a servant or someone who worships out of obligation, but as a child who adores his father.

Today, let's approach worship with the heart of a child, pouring out our love on our Heavenly Father.

HEART QUESTIONS TO PONDER:

Am I able to view God as a loving father in my life?

How can I get back to a child-like wonder and amazement
in my worship?

16

DAILY DECISIONS I JOHNATHAN GROAN

Johnathan shares his gift of music by leading the Heart of Worship band fearlessly. He plays the bass and has mentored many young musicians.

Multitudes, multitudes in the valley of decision:
for the day of the LORD is near in the valley of decision.
(Joel 3:14) KJV

So many decisions! Our lives are shaped by the decisions that we make every single day. If you've seen a "healthy" person, then you could guess that they decided to eat…a wealthy person decided to work hard…a poor person decided not to work …an educated person decided to study…a Christian decided to believe… and on and on.

As you can see, decisions determine our destination! They shape our circumstances, beliefs, attitude, personality, and the core being of who we are. The good news? We are able to change our current destination at any moment if we aren't pleased with the path we're on. Our decisions will ultimately determine our eternal destination. Therefore, I believe it's wise to align our decisions with the Word of God. It contains the answers to all of our questions and promises eternal life if we make the right decisions.

Joshua 24:15 gives the instruction: *"And if it is evil in your eyes to serve the Lord, choose this day whom you will serve…"* The Israelites had to choose whether or not they would serve the Lord.

We must do the same. We do this in determining to obey the commandments listed in the Word of God. Obedience demonstrates our love for Him! John 14:15 declares "If ye love me, keep my commandments".

Every day we should ask ourselves, *'is this decision in agreement with the Word of God?'* This is easier to do when we become eternally minded rather than carnally minded.

We often make decisions complicated. However, we can simplify our decision process.

> *But seek ye first the kingdom of God,*
> *and His righteousness;*
> *and all these things shall be added unto you.*
> Matthew 6:33 (KJV)

This means, if we will put God's kingdom and righteousness first through obedience, He'll guide us through life with blessings, miracles, and answers to the hard questions. Cast aside unbelief so He can do great things through us and for us.

The Bible records many accounts of miracles that were fulfilled because someone made a decision to trust.

In Mark 7:26-29, a Greek woman begged Jesus to cast a devil out of her daughter. Jesus attempted to defer her with an insult. He said, "… it is not meet to take the children's bread and cast it unto dogs." Could you imagine Jesus, the God of love, comparing you a dog? However, the woman kept a good attitude. She humbled herself and said to Him, "Yes Lord; yet the dogs under the table eat of the children's crumbs". As a result of this one decision, her daughter received her miracle.

So, our choices matter and they determine every aspect of our lives. Today is the day to start making daily decisions that lead us into eternal life.

HEART QUESTIONS TO PONDER:

Does the Bible direct my daily decisions?
Or are they based on how I feel in the moment?

What decisions have I made in my life that were not aligned with Biblical teachings? What would I do differently if faced with the same choice today?

LIVING WORSHIP | KARLA HOLLEY

Karla is the Pastor's wife and Worship Pastor at Life Church in Wichita Falls, Texas. She has been leading worship in churches and conferences for many years. Karla has a passion for prayer and people.

*"Though the fig tree should not blossom
and there be no fruit on the vines,
though the yield of the olive should fail
and the fields produce no food,
though the flock should be cut off from the fold
and there be no cattle in the stalls,
Yet I will exult in the Lord, I will rejoice in the God of my salvation."*
(Habakkuk 3:17-18) NASB

"Living worship" means all of life. Everything we do and say is an act of worship when we do it as unto the Lord.

As a girl and young teenager, I remember hearing my Mother quietly say, "Thank you, Jesus" or "I love you, Jesus" and sometimes even a "Hallelujah!" I'm not talking about when we were in the middle of a worship service. This might happen anywhere around our home, walking through the grocery store or driving in the car. My Dad often did the same kind of thing. While driving down the road, I would hear a hearty, "Hallelujah!" come from driver's seat.

My husband, Gene, tells of how his grandfather would walk through the grocery store and worship as he went. Gene and his cousins would get embarrassed and try to get him to be quieter, but that usually encouraged him to continue worshiping at the same volume… and sometimes even a little louder.

Looking back on those times, I now realize my parents and Gene's grandfather were simply living worship. Worship for them was not just limited to a church building. Worship became who they were. They worshiped even in places a child or teenager might see as inappropriate. However, they recognized the limitlessness of His power and could – and would – worship wherever they were.

When I consider the phrase "*living worship*", I see it two ways. First, worship is alive. It's something that is active. It's not dead, dull and boring. I'm thankful to experience lively worship with church family on a weekly basis. Secondly, I see worship as a lifestyle. We should live in a spirit of worship as my parents & Gene's grandfather demonstrated. I want to challenge us all to reach toward this lifestyle of worship.

Worship is not restricted to one location or building. Anytime we step into an act of service, we worship. Service is worship and worship glorifies God. 1 Peter 4:11 (NRSV) says, "*Whoever speaks must do so as one speaking the very words of God; whoever serves must do so with the strength that God supplies, so that God may be glorified in all things…*" God will receive glory from our acts of service. Nothing is insignificant.

As worship leaders, each time we step off the platform we have an opportunity to continue to our live out our worship in the context of life. We live our worship when we help those who are widowed, orphaned or imprisoned. We live our worship when we privately do good for someone, share our testimony with an unbeliever, or take time to pray with someone. This *is* living worship.

It is so important that we live what we sing. Worship should not be restricted to special seasons or days of celebration. We live worship moment by moment, day by day in the presence of the Lord, honoring Him in our hearts. We must be open to allowing God to awe us in the everyday - the laughter of a child, a beautiful sunset, a cool ocean breeze, crisp morning rain or the touch of someone you love.

Leading worship requires an ongoing relationship with Jesus. The role of a worship leader is not primarily musical. It is first and foremost, spiritual. You will not be able to effectively lead worship over the long-term if you do not have a personal relationship with God, because you cannot take people where you have not been.

I challenge you to live worship behind closed doors when it's only you and Him. It's in those moments when you're working through a set for the next service that all of a sudden you will feel the strong presence of God. Or maybe you're listening… and listening… and listening to find the next "right" song to teach your team, and the presence of God sweeps over you. These are moments when you are living worship.

Live worship in your church community. Live it in your city. Live your worship in your schools… at the office… in the grocery store… at Starbucks. Don't wait for a church service or even a churchy place. Find some private space and let your worship begin to flow. Let your life be *"living worship"* to Him in all you do. Just worship!

HEART QUESTIONS TO PONDER:

Am I living worship everyday or just going through the motions of leading worship on Sunday?

Am I worshiping at all times or only when circumstances are the way I want them to be?

PRAY MORE THAN YOU PRACTICE | BOBBIE SHOEMAKE

Bobbie has written classic songs that the Church has sung for many years. She continues to inspire many and lead worship throughout North America.

---

*When You said, 'Seek My face,'
My heart said to You,
'Your face, Lord, I will seek.'
(Psalm 27:8) NKJV*

In my travels I have observed that many worship leaders are serving with sincerity but have not created their own private consecration time. If worship leaders have not developed a private relationship with God that focuses on personal times of worship, they will be unable to lead an authentic worship experience in public or expect to lead an anointed worship service. Personal preparation creates confidence in our ability to be Spirit led.

Today we are in a spiritual battle. Worship teams are the front line of attack. However, not everyone is prepared for the battle. The praise team rehearses and prepares to be excellent in performance, but we need our praise teams to practice prayer and to practice worship as much, or more, than they practice songs.

In the Old Testament, King Jehoshaphat (2 Chronicles 20: 5-27) appointed singers to lead the army, proclaiming the magnificence and holiness of God. As they worshiped, God caused confusion in the enemy army and a great victory was won that day.

If worship leaders and teams will pray more than they practice, there will be a flow in the Holy Ghost. God will provide the excellence of anointing that we want and need. If we give ourselves to Him, He will give us the desires of our heart. It is not unusual for personal worship sessions to lead to divine inspiration and creative impartation. Anointed songs can be released while we worship.

Although it is helpful to be current in our song choices and musically proficient, what the congregation really needs is to feel a God Connection. Everyone is busy, and our time is complicated with the demands of what seems to be urgent. As worshipers and worship leaders we must recognize that what often seems to be urgent is much less important than simply returning to the basics – we are called to be worshipers of God. Our first call is to be worshipers of God in our personal lives, not to stand before a congregation. We cannot direct or choreograph people into the presence of God with our words. It is through our own heart of worship that we are able to lead others.

One of the most valuable things we can do to develop spiritual sensitivity is to find a mentor – a prayer warrior, a spirit directed worship leader, 'seasoned' saint – someone who has a consistent spiritual life and knows the ways of the Spirit of God. Make spending time in prayer and worship with this mentor a priority. Some things are better caught than taught.

If we desire to be spiritually sensitive and quick to recognize the moving of the Spirit, it is necessary to spend time alone worshiping. This time should be devoted to encountering the Presence of God. Worship leaders who do not practice the presence of the Lord will overlook 'moments' of spiritual importance because they are focused on the plan more than the voice of God. "Flow" cannot be taught - it must be lived.

Perhaps these thoughts will lead some of us to reevaluate what we do and how we do it. Have we allowed a performance focus to displace our first call? Are we letting the time required to learn and teach new material take the place of face-to-face worship?

Take time today to set aside every distraction, and to focus on God while singing or playing your instrument. Linger in His presence, listen to His voice.

HEART QUESTIONS TO PONDER:

The anointing will break whatever yoke there may be in each service. Is my church experiencing 'yoke-breaking' anointed worship on a regular basis?

Am I confident enough in my ability to hear the voice of God to use a "Spirit-directed" song if it is not on the list?

19

MORE THAN A MUSICIAN I ANDY FERGUSON

Andy is the full-grown version of a guitar prodigy. He and his wife, Heather, are Worship Pastors at Gate City United Pentecostal Church in Gate City, VA. He is a gifted songwriter, recording artist, anointed worship leader and preacher.

> *So the men of Kiriath-jearim came to get the Ark of the Lord. They took it to the hillside home of Abinadab and ordained Eleazar, his son, to be in charge of it.*
> *(I Samuel 7:1) NLT*

We serve an omnipresent God, He occupies all time and space, all seeing and knowing. He's the Alpha and Omega, beginning and the end. When we begin to worship, we open the door to connect with an eternal, all-powerful God.

Imagine a room full of people where someone is experiencing a medical emergency. Immediately we search for a doctor, the one person who can capably manage the crisis. Then, when the doctor arrives, everyone steps back while the physician addresses the need.

So it is with God. He is already present in the room. As we begin to seek Him in worship, and magnify Him on our instruments, we call God forward into His role. Our worship brings attention to Him. God is then able to perform and do what only He can do. When we step back, God can step up to save, heal, and deliver. This is why healings can happen during a song or hearts are transformed during a worship service.

Music can take us back to our childhood or remind us of someone we love. It enhances our memory of a moment in time; that's why most special occasions have some celebratory song to go with it.

Musicians can set an emotional mood or atmosphere, just because of the power of music itself. Yet being a great musician does not bring the focus on God. Instead, your musicianship will bring the attention to whatever you are carrying in your heart.

There is nothing more powerful than a musician that comprehends when his musical talent needs to "step back" and allow the Great Physician to take preeminence. When a musician chooses to use their gifting this way, earth literally connects to heaven.

In the same way that Eleazar was asked to keep the ark of the covenant in 1 Sam. 7:1, we should also choose, as musicians, to be the keeper of the sacred things of God. Eleazar was sanctified (the New Living Translation says he was ordained) to keep the ark, which is a representation of the presence of God.

Likewise, we are sanctified to carry God's presence. From service to service we are to carry His glory. In prayer we are to seek for the songs, melodies, and rhythms that will connect the congregation to His presence.

> *For if the trumpet give an uncertain sound,*
> *who shall prepare himself to the battle?*
> (1 Corinthians 14:8) KJV

It is imperative we keep our heart pure, our skill sharp and always stay prepared for whatever we may face. This is why rehearsals are more than musical run-throughs! If we are leaders of any kind, whether that be band leader, worship leader or the administrative leader of our music team, we should come to weekly rehearsal with a glimpse of where God is taking us and our team. Rehearsal is not a time to focus on music only, but it's an opportunity to rehearse God's plan and re-see it while in rehearsal. Always remember the musicians go first in the battle. We need to stay prepared mind, body and soul. Without sanctification and preparation, we will only carry our humanity, which will lead to confusion.

Our purpose is to honor the house of God, live in repentance, walk in humility, and serve in reverence. No matter the style of music or the instrument we play, our identity in Christ must be prevalent. We are more than musicians; we carry the King of Glory in our hearts and entertain Him with the gift that He has given us while encouraging others to follow our example. Our music is the call for the Alpha and Omega to step into the room.

HEART QUESTIONS TO PONDER:

Is it possible to bring the emotion of music into the room without actually ushering the presence of God into the room?
How do I make sure this is not happening in my own music ministry?

How do I rehearse God's plan for a service and not just prepare the musical side of things?

20

PRACTICING THE PRESENCE OF THE LORD I
MARLO SPIDLE

Marlo has a heart for leading and mentoring young people. As Minister of Music, she uses her education and experience to pour eternal principles into the people attending The Apostolic Center in Matoon, IL.

> *So they brought the ark of God,*
> *and set it in the midst of the tent that David had pitched for it:*
> *and they offered burnt sacrifices and peace offerings before God.*
> *And when David had made an end of offering the*
> *burnt offerings and the peace offerings,*
> *he blessed the people in the name of the LORD.*
> *...And he appointed certain of the Levites to minister before the ark of the LORD,*
> *and to record, and to thank and praise the LORD God of Israel...*
> (1 Chronicles 16:1-5) KJV

When I was a young girl, I was taught a life changing principle. At the time, I didn't realize that I was being "*taught,*" but, looking back, every opportunity was taken to instill this principle within me. It simply is to "practice the presence of the Lord."

Being raised in a pastor's home with my mother as the music director, I was always around some type of "practicing" in my home or church. Whether on the piano, bass, drums, saxophone or vocals, we were encouraged to prepare ourselves for the musical task or event. I only began to realize the importance of the underlying lesson as I grew older. Every opportunity to practice was given substance and power by God's presence. You see, it's not enough to play or sing well. Invoking the Redeemer of the song must be woven into each moment of personal preparation.

I Chronicles chapter 16 recounts the story of how David organized worship in the temple. In verse 5 the people responsible for worship are named: Asaph (*Gatherer/Collector*), Zechariah (*God has Remembered*), Jeie (*God Sweeps Away*), Shemiramoth (*Name of Heights*), Jehiel (*Carried Away of God*), Mattihiah (*Gift of God*), Eliab (*My God is My Father*), Benaiah (*God has Built Up*), and Obed-edom (*Servant of Edom, Now Redeemed*).

I find it interesting that the worshipers, who were the most skilled in the land, all had a specific relationship with God and a reason to participate in worship, except for Asaph. However, the last phrase of verse 5 says "but Asaph made a sound with cymbals". These cymbals were "loud-sounding cymbals," - intended to get the attention of the people and to proclaim or announce.

This word is used in the same manner in Isaiah to describe God's messengers.

> How lovely on the mountains
> are the feet of him who brings good news,
> who announces peace and brings good news of happiness,
> who announces salvation, and says to Zion,
> Your God reigns!
> (Isaiah 52:7) KJV

As part of the sacrificial worship, when the burnt offering occurred, the priests gave three blasts on trumpets, then the head of the Levites clashed the cymbals (James W. McKinnom). The response to this playing of cymbals (*or announcement*) was worship. I am intrigued by the idea of Asaph. He was the head musician, and was responsible for the worship service, the planning and the practicing. And he played the cymbals.

Asaph's name meant gatherer or collector. Could it be that his most important job was to announce or proclaim the goodness of God and gather everyone to worship? The responsibility to practice the presence of God rested in his hands.

When running a vocal or musical practice, when we pray, God automatically is with us. But when we begin to "practice His presence" something deeper happens. The spirit of the room changes; it becomes a teaching moment to those that are attending the practice. I stop and announce the moment - inviting those at the practice to recognize His presence as the approval of the practice and plan. Recognizing His presence and "leaning" into it requires an understanding of the moving and direction of the Spirit of God.

As a singer, musician or worship leader, it is imperative to take advantage of these moments. But it's also imperative that we teach the next generation to recognize these God moments. So often we assume that those we lead have the same experience with the presence of God or His anointing, as ourselves. But in Psalms 145:4 we are admonished, "*One generation shall praise thy works to another, and shall declare thy mighty acts.*"

Recently, I was at a retreat where the speaker spoke about Deborah, the judge, whose name means "bee". The message focused on the verse in Judges 5:12: "*Awake, awake, Deborah: awake, awake, utter a song: arise, Barak, and lead thy captivity captive, thou son of Abinoam.*"

The speaker addressed the current crisis in the bee community. It is called Colony Collapse Disorder (CCD). This disorder has come about because there are no worker bees to teach the younger bees how to work.

Deborah was willing to recognize the moment, to seize the opportunity and make a difference. Deborah tells Barak, "Get up for this IS the day - the Lord has already gone out before us." Israel won the victory that day because Deborah took advantage of a "God Moment."

How many of us are creating a colony that is going to collapse? What are our priorities? Wow! - Awake, AWAKE vocalist, musician, leader - sing the song, announce, declare, proclaim the goodness of God! It is time for every generation to practice HIS presence.

HEART QUESTIONS TO PONDER:

A quote by J. Wolfendale says, *"Song - a power for which its possessors are responsible."* What is "my song?"
Am I transferring it to the next generation?

How can I actively practice the presence of the Lord in rehearsal this week?

Choose a song from your upcoming Sunday set and practice the presence of God without worrying about performance.

21

LEADERSHIP THROUGH SERVANTHOOD I SHAWN BIGBY

Shawn is a Worship Pastor and gospel recording artist who has been serving the Kingdom of God in churches and conferences for many years. He is a songwriter and dynamic teacher on worship and the sacred responsibility of the worship leader.

> *I want to know Christ and experience the mighty power
> that raised him from the dead.
> ...I don't mean to say that I have already achieved
> these things or that I have already reached perfection.
> But I press on to possess that perfection
> for which Christ Jesus first possessed me.
> No, dear brothers and sisters, I have not achieved it,
> but I focus on this one thing:
> Forgetting the past and looking forward to what lies ahead,
> I press on to reach the end of the race
> and receive the heavenly prize for which God,
> through Christ Jesus, is calling us.*
> (Philippians 3:10-14) NLT

I recently watched a documentary of the life of Quincy Jones. I was COMPLETELY enamored and amazed by his story. This man was literally at the forefront of the last 60-plus years of music. He was not hampered by styles or genres but instead embraced music in its totality no matter the presentation or package it was presented in. From his early years, and throughout a lifetime in the music industry, Quincy Jones never ceased to be a student.

What I appreciated most about his story is something he shared about hip hop music. He didn't grow up listening to it nor was it his favorite form of music, but when he noticed that it was taking the music industry and culture by storm, he determined to learn more about it. He sought out hip hop artists and chose to learn from them. He broke the music down into a form he could understand, apply and produce.

Picture this. Quincy Jones, a man responsible for producing Oscar and Grammy award winning works such as *The Color Purple*, *Thriller*, and *We Are The World*; was now sitting at the feet of young, upstart artists. These young artists didn't have the accolades, clout, or longevity of Quincy Jones. What they did have was the ear and pulse of the current culture. Oh, did I mention, Quincy was in his 60's, when he decided to learn a brand new way of musical presentation and interpretation?

When you are a leader it can be very easy to get to a place where you feel "my way has been successful so therefore my way is THE way." Sometimes we are tempted by the thought, "I have arrived so everyone else should do it my way!" If we're not careful, SUCCESS becomes an enemy of leadership.

In Philippians, Paul was essentially laying out his resume to the church of Philippi. He starts by talking about how deeply entrenched as a Hebrew he was and how legitimate his heritage was. He boasts of his Jewish accomplishments and rank. Then detours and talks about his post-Jesus transformation. He talks about what he has learned and how he desires to learn more about this Jesus who has saved him. Paul willingly admits that he hasn't gotten "there" yet.

What an example! Paul was a leader willing to admit that even though he had accomplished so much, at the end of the day, he had not learned or done it all! Paul says "I press on...." He challenges us all to keep going. Why? Because the end of the race isn't dictated by us; it is dictated by the One for whom we race.

As a leader you should NEVER stop learning. Technology, culture, music, people, life. All of these things change and evolve! If you don't believe me....try downloading Planning Center to one of the old gray-scale Nokia cell phones! Leaders have to keep themselves in a posture to learn and improve.

Sometimes it is as simple as finding a younger or older person in your church and having a conversation with them. You will be amazed at what they may share that you had NO clue about. Surround yourself with people who are more talented, more gifted, more experienced than you in certain areas and take in what they give out. There is an old saying that fits in here: "if you are the biggest fish in your pond, then it's possible you need another pond."

HEART QUESTIONS TO PONDER:

When I look at my surroundings, do I perceive myself to be the "biggest fish" in my pond? If so, what kind of people do I need to surround myself with so I can grow?

What unknown topic could I read about, study, listen to, or research that would help me become a better leader?

Are there any areas of success I am no longer willing or challenged to grow in?

22

FOLLOW TO LEAD I KELLEE HOPPER

Kellee is an anointed worship leader and songwriter. In the workforce, she is a corporate executive. As Music Ministry Director at Revival Center in Modesto, CA, she faithfully demonstrates servant leadership.

> *Follow my example, as I follow the example of Christ.*
> *(I Corinthians 11:1) NIV*

> *For as many as are led by the Spirit of God,*
> *they are the sons of God.*
> (Romans 8:14) KJV

A few months ago, I read a statement that said "Worship leading is really just…. worship following." I was so impacted by this that it became a devotional for our music team. How many times have I looked at what our music team does in a service as worship leading? I know I've been guilty of saying "I have to lead worship today" or asking someone if they were leading worship. While well-intentioned, this phrase, so easily understood in our community, sets up a narrative that is wrong. Granted, we want our actions to actively demonstrate worship to those in attendance, and we usually are the first to worship outwardly during a service. Yet I realize the more appropriate description of what we should strive for is "worship following."

The best leaders are intentional followers and passionate pursuers of God's glory. They understand the goal of a worship experience is to deliberately pursue the heart of God, and allow Him to lead us to the place where His presence surrounds us, His glory permeates the sanctuary, and His will has preeminence over anything and everything. Our efforts are most effective and spiritually impactful when we let God do the worship leading and we follow His direction, when we let His will take priority over our agenda, and when we allow His voice to be heard and ours silenced.

I Corinthians 1:29 (KJV) reminds us "*No flesh should glory in His presence.*" The platform should never be a stage to display individual talents and abilities. We must not be deceived into thinking we are the reason for a response from the congregation. God may choose to use us as instruments of praise but we are not the conductor – He is! In those supernatural moments, the platform ceases to become a stage or a spotlight opportunity. The temptation for self-glory and attention is erased. The carnal focus on "performance" is gone. Instead, we find ourselves saturated by His presence. At those times, it truly becomes a "heaven touching earth" moment.

The beautiful thing is, when we recognize Him as the Supreme Leader and we as followers, we actually become joined with Him in the process. Romans 8:14 proclaims, when we are led by His Spirit, we have the promise of being relationally connected to Him, to the point that He calls us His children! What a wonderful thought that is!

So, to the human eye, it might look like we are "worship leading" in a church service, when in reality, we should be on a continuous quest to "worship follow." We actively pursue the presence of the One who so deserves our praise, adoration and worship. When that happens, we show others the way to "follow the Leader."

HEART QUESTIONS TO PONDER:

As a worshipper, what physical and spiritual examples
can I emulate so others see that I am following Christ,
as referenced in I Corinthians 11:1?

How do I know that I am following in worship,
rather than operating in the mechanics of leading worship?

How can I better prepare myself and my team to maintain a posture
of worship-following while leading worship in a service?

23

THE "WHY" OF EXCELLENCE I CAM COOK

Cameron is 19 years old and a musical prodigy. He has been playing at The Pentecostals of Alexandria, LA since he was 12 and is on a path to full time ministry.

> *And whatsoever ye do, do it heartily,*
> *as to the Lord, and not unto men;*
> *Knowing that of the Lord ye shall receive*
> *the reward of the inheritance: for ye serve the Lord Christ.*
> *But he that doeth wrong shall receive for the wrong*
> *which he hath done: and there is no respect of persons.*
> *(Colossians 3:23-25) KJV*

In today's world, it is so easy to settle for shortcuts or short-term wins in order to appear we have it all together. Why work hard when you can make everyone THINK you work hard? Like an addict, we lackadaisically walk through life searching for the next "high" of the approval we receive when we appear to be winning in ministry or life. It is hard not to fall into the trap of working for the acceptance of others instead of working for the approval of God. To be fair, the former has a much more expedient profit. However, I believe God has called us to have a deeper view of *why* we work and *why* we should require excellence.

In his book *Start With Why*, Simon Sinek continually uses the phrase, "People don't buy WHAT you do, they buy WHY you do it." At the core of what we do, we must first know why we do what we do. Once we know why, it is much easier to put hard work behind the task. The Bible gives us a perfect way to view our work.

In Colossians 3:23, it says to "do it heartily." The word heartily is described as "with zest or gusto" and "wholly, thoroughly." In my mind, that definition encompasses the true meaning of excellence. This proves that God has called us to do whatever we do *with excellence.*

Knowing that God has called us to this, we need to evaluate how to go about accomplishing things with excellence. As was stated in the reference scripture, work can be done as to the Lord or unto men. Knowing the two options of excellence, it takes asking yourself some hard questions to know which side you stand on. We must daily check our motives. Why am I pursuing this idea? For my good or for His glory? Am I settling for quick results or am I daily choosing to work for the "reward of the inheritance"? We know there is an eternal reward for work done unto the Lord. *Daily* decisions to choose excellence over laziness lead to a *life* of excellence, which God then receives as worship.

> *It was by faith that Abel*
> *brought a more acceptable offering to God than Cain did.*
> *Abel's offering gave evidence that he was a righteous man,*
> *and God showed his approval of his gifts.*
> *Although Abel is long dead,*
> *he still speaks to us by his example of faith.*
> Hebrews 11:4 (NLT)

God accepted Abel's sacrifice because his offering was evidence he was righteous. I believe God sees our sacrifice/offering (hard work in this case) before he sees who it is giving the offering. Colossians states, "there is no respect of persons." God saw the heart behind each sacrifice. Cain's motives were eventually revealed when his sacrifice was not accepted. Instead of reflecting on the *why* behind his sacrifice, he succumbed to the envious human nature and killed his brother. We must purify our motives and assess our *why* of excellence before God can ever receive our sacrifice.

Before we take action on whatever it is we are trying to accomplish, we should first know why we do something, and for whom we do it. Knowing the source of our reward gives us the confidence and vision needed to work with excellence and complete the task. Once those motives are analyzed and clear, GO! No matter how big or small the task may be, DO!

Many times, we wait on God to bless something before we "go all in". We hold back our time or resources, waiting to know if God is "in something". In reality, God is waiting on us to act on our faith before He blesses it. He can only bless what is already there!

> *He that is faithful in that which is least*
> *is faithful also in much:*
> *and he that is unjust in the least*
> *is unjust also in much,*
> Luke 16:10 (KJV)

If God can trust us to be committed and excellent in what is least, it will grow. He will trust us with more, but first we must *do* our part in the little things.

Today, I can encourage you to CHOOSE EXCELLENCE, knowing God honors hard work done unto Him. Be faithful in that which is least so He can trust you to be faithful in much!

HEART QUESTIONS TO PONDER:

Am I daily pursuing excellence?

Am I working as to the Lord or unto men?

Am I seeking excellence for an expedient profit
or an eternal reward?

24

WORSHIP AND OUR RELATIONSHIP WITH JESUS | CHARITY GAYLE

Charity's passion for God's presence is felt through the incredible roster of songs she has written. Weekly she leads people on many platforms throughout the world into the presence of God.

> *It is good to give thanks to the Lord,*
> *to sing praises to the Most High.*
> *It is good to proclaim your unfailing love*
> *in the morning, your faithfulness in the evening.*
> *(Psalm 92:1-2) NLT*

I think we get tripped up on the word worship sometimes. To some, it's only meaning to sing a song on a Sunday morning at church or simply offer an outward expression of praise like lifting your hands or shouting *"Hallelujah!"* Now, these things can be a piece of worship, but to make things a little clearer, let's replace the word *worship* with the word *love*.

I have recently fallen in love and gotten married. If there's one thing I know, it is this: the relationship I have with Ryan is deeper than I can describe. However, it wouldn't have gotten that way if I didn't communicate with him. I know it sounds simple, but *that* is how God wants to relate to us.

From the beginning of mankind, all God has wanted is to be with us! He seeks us. He pursues a real and genuine relationship with His creation. But we messed up. We wanted knowledge more than we wanted God, and this choice caused a barrier between us.

However, God didn't give up on us easily. He committed the greatest act of love by putting on flesh and dying for our sins so we could have access to Him once again. Now that's true love.

If I only tended to my relationship with Ryan by talking to him a couple of hours a week, our marriage would fall apart. It wasn't until I had this realization about my relationship with the Lord that I came to understand I hadn't really experienced what I could in my relationship with Jesus. He wants to spend time with me. He wants me to tell Him how good He is. He wants me to cast all of my cares on Him.

My husband has written me love songs. He takes his love and pens it into lyrics and melody. There's something about that creativity coupled with his love for me that makes my heart melt. However, if he only professed his love to me in a song, and never spoke to me otherwise, it would not be a good thing. Do you see? Can you understand why the Lord adores our worship through song but why it needs to be - must be - more than that?

I love the song that says "I'm coming back to the *Heart* of Worship // and it's all about *You*." Worship is more than a song. It isn't genuine if it isn't all about the Lord. Period.

It's not about how great a singer or musician someone is, how great a platform your gift provides, or the song that's being sung. If our worship isn't expressing how much we love him, it's just a show. Music is not our object of worship, it's merely a tool we use to express our adoration for God.

Let's look at Psalm 92, which is currently one of my favorite psalms. First of all, this scripture validates the role of music in worship: "*It is GOOD to make music to your name O Most High* (vs 1). Secondly, it is David's proclamation of God's love and faithfulness: "*Proclaiming your love in the morning and your faithfulness at night*" (vs 2). When I look at that scripture, I see daily adoration to

God. Our worship needs to be abundant, whether with music, praise, or simply talking with God.

When I was little, worship was taught to me as giving thanks and love to the Lord. No matter what song was being sung (even if it wasn't a song I 'preferred'), I lifted my hands, I showed the Lord I loved Him through what I knew to be praise. Now that I'm older I understand that everyday He is the same, so everyday my worship should be the same also. Worship is talking to Jesus while I do the dishes, Worship is doing my best to love my neighbor. Worship is being like Jesus and giving hope to all, whether we agree with them or not.

Do we want to worship the Lord deeper? Put worship in the context of God's love. Build a stronger relationship with God by a daily lifestyle of worship. Allow your worship to be one of the ways you communicate and draw closer to your Creator.

Let's *really* love Him through our worship.

HEART QUESTIONS TO PONDER:

Do I fall in the rut of only worshiping God through song?
I will set a goal for this week to worship him personally
without music playing or performing music for Him.

In what way am I getting to know God through his Word?
How is this different than just reading the Word of God?

WORSHIP
SEASONS

25

THE MIRACULOUS WAYMAKER | KARA WILLIAMS

Kara is a worship leader, wife, mother and full-time educator. She has served faithfully for over twenty years on the music ministry team of The Pentecostals of Alexandria LA. Her voice has been heard all over the world.

> *Wait patiently for the Lord. Be brave and courageous.*
> *Yes, wait patiently for the Lord.*
> (Psalm 27:14) NLT

More than a decade ago, while recovering from a traumatic life change, I boldly told the devil that he "would have to do better than that" if he was going to take me down. He definitely heard me. So began the trial of my life. The test of all tests... the one that would make me question everything. Who am I? Who is God? What do I believe? Is any of this real? Does any of it matter? What is wrong with me? This journey would force me to learn how to *really* pray, *really* trust God, and *really* .... wait.

I have laughed (and cried) many times at the cartoon that randomly circulates on social media: "I don't have time for the nervous breakdown I deserve."

Do you ever wish that you could press pause on your life? I know I do. I am so desperate for a miracle that I just want to spend every waking moment praying.....or fasting....or maybe even just sleeping. However my kids won't understand why I need a break from being Mom for a while. The housework and the bills surely will not wait. My job likely won't be there anymore if I don't show up for a few weeks. I wonder who of my friends will be there patiently waiting when I come back out of hiding? So, I press on, whispering to God, "*I am still here…waiting…*" while struggling to maintain my many roles.

Somewhere along this journey, at Because of the Times 2018, I was given a song to lead. I liked the song and I knew it would go over well with the crowd. I wish I could say I knew it would be such a hit. Had I known, I might would have spent a little more time on my hair that night or something.

I wish I could share the feedback, the testimonies, the stories, the messages I have received…..unreal stories of people just like me and you that need desperately to be reminded God is in control. I have received messages from people locally, nationally and internationally… Christians, non-Christians, atheists, and other denominations. To this day I rarely go into Target without someone yelling down the aisle, "Hey! Aren't you the *Waymaker* Lady?".

If you know me, you know I am extremely uncomfortable with this amount of attention. In addition to that fact, I felt like a fraud. If I am singing this, and getting so much recognition, shouldn't I have something to back it up? Shouldn't I have some profound words to say when people ask me to take a picture with them? I believe it…I think. I mean, I believe it most of the time. I believe it while I am singing. Ok, I am trying to believe it. Maybe if I sing it enough times, I will truly believe.

I know God can do anything…but will He? Ok, He will…but maybe not for me. If God is going to come through for me, would make me wait *this* long?

Needless to say, I have wrestled with my faith terribly. But, I have settled on this: This is not my song. These are not my words. I didn't add the prophetic stanza at the end….."even when I don't see it, you're working...". But, it is my desperate plea for God to be and do all those things. Those lyrics are my declaration, my reminder, my landmark, the cornerstone of my sanity at this point. God is in control. His ways are higher than mine. He sees what I don't see. He knows what I don't know. He *is* working. Stop trying to fix it, Kara. Stop trying to understand why.....trust God...and *wait*.

Isn't it funny how God works? The Pentecostals of Alexandria support staff at the POA continue to forward messages to me. These messages are from people who testify that they watch *Waymaker* when they feel hopeless. Without fail, I receive the messages in a moment when I feel like I cannot take another step forward, when my own faith is at rock bottom, and when I feel hopeless. The messages used to make me feel uncomfortable, but now they have become like manna. They are little nuggets of strength in this time of waiting and seeking God.

Millions of views....and it was really just for *me*. Every testimony represents people who, in the midst of waiting for their miracle, have found reassurance in those declarative lyrics...God is the Waymaker. The Miracle Worker. The Promise Keeper.

God is faithful.

Even when you don't see it, He is working.

Just... *wait*.

HEART QUESTIONS TO PONDER:

How do we continue to lead publicly when faith
feels tested by trials?

Has God ever used me to declare His greatness over a situation
while I was still struggling? What have I learned from these
moments?

26

WEARINESS OF THE JOURNEY I KAREN HARDING

Karen is a powerfully anointed songwriter, singer, and preacher. She ministers worldwide and is a woman of great faith. Goodlettsville Pentecostal Church is her home base when she isn't out "giving Jesus to the world".

And let us not grow weary in well doing
for in due season we shall reap, if we faint not!
Galatians 6:9 (KJV)

Are you tired? Afraid of burn-out?? Take time to read this and be encouraged to *never* give up! You *will* make it!! Just keep going! Here are some thoughts to help you along this journey.

Consider this... I'm writing this the day after returning from South Africa. I've been through eighteen hours of tiresome travel and ten days of intense spiritual warfare. Am I weary? In body, yes. In Spirit? *Never.*

Are you feeling worn out and tired? Are you not seeing the results you expected? Perhaps you haven't reached the place you thought you would be soon enough? God cares about your rest.

God has told his people,
'Here is a place of rest; let the weary rest here.
This is a place of quiet rest.'
Isaiah 28:12 (NLT)

Let's take a look at some practical things you can do to find rest.

Give yourself permission to rest. Take a day of reflection. Sometimes you just need an hour alone with no outside noise or influence. Turn on the diffuser with lavender calming oils or light your favorite scented candle. Drink a cup of your favorite beverage. Chose to be *alone*!! Breathe in…breathe out.

Other times you may need a little more time away. A short get-away. The definition of away is "removed from a particular thing, place or position "

Rest also comes by reviving our spirit, not just our body. Get in the word and find a posture of restful prayer! Meditate on God's provision and goodness.

> *"The Lord is my strength and my shield.*
> *My heart trusted in Him and I am helped.*
> *Therefore my heart greatly rejoiceth*
> *and with my song will I praise Him*
> (Psalms 28:7) KJV

Rest and replenish, but never quit. Keep going, keep pressing on. . I admit at times I think, *Why am I doing this? Will I ever see results? Will things ever change? Is it really worth the effort?* The answer is yes. A thousand times yes!

> *I press toward the mark*
> *of the high calling of God in Christ Jesus*
> (Philippians 3:4) KJV

If one soul hears a song, a note, a word, and they are touched, changed or encouraged then, yes, it is worth it. We must remember why we do what we do. We are called to serve God's kingdom. To minister means to attend to the wants or needs of others; this reminder should help us push past our weariness.

With that being said... to minister you must fill yourself up first. Then you have strength to help others. This thing called ministry can get very heavy at times. It's not for the faint of heart! It can be tiresome and a huge load to carry. However, the rewards of the end result make it worth the fight!

Sometimes our battles are physical. Other times, we face an emotional or mental battle. Regardless, keep fighting the good fight. It is so worth the struggle!

Will everyone love every song you sing?? No, but keep singing. Does everyone realize all the hard work you do? Probably not. Keep pressing and keep working. Many times in the middle of exhaustion and weariness I've walked to the podium, picked up the microphone and began singing truths - lines of songs that encourage and restore lost hope and faith. And something remarkable happened. In the middle of ministering to others, I began to feel a surge of power, God's strength and energy flowing into me. Ah! *The joy of the Lord is my strength!* I was simply using the gift that God had put in my hands.

David used his harp and a slingshot. Evil spirits departed when David played and worshiped. Lions, bears and a giant named Goliath were killed because David was comfortable using what God had placed in his hands. Use your talent!

Back your talent up with prayer and let strength flow into your weary soul. A fresh anointing will empower your gift. It's more than a song; it's a message of hope and encouragement. The songs you sing and play are ordained as a lifting.

We gain strength when we connect with peers, music friends or ministry friends who understand our battles, the challenges and rewards of ministry. We need people that will speak encouragement into our lives. It helps to know we are not in this alone. It is a comfort to be affirmed with words such as: "*I'm praying for you,"* or *"You've got this!"* or *"I believe in you"*. These moments of hope can make all the difference in the world!

Be a lifter not a leaner.
Be an encourager!
Be a "crown-polisher".
Be someone's cheering section.
Acknowledge the accomplishments of others and celebrate them.

When we encourage others, it becomes the perfect antidote to our weariness.

Realize God loves us. He loves our worship. His desire is for us to operate our ministries with joy and confidence. Let's raise our hands in worship. Never quit. Find rest, but never let it remove us from what God ordained us to do in His kingdom. We will keep pressing on!! The rewards are so worth it!. You *can* do this, and you are not alone

Rest.
Repeat...

HEART QUESTIONS TO PONDER:

What three things will help me endure despite the weariness of the journey?

Will I allow myself time and permission to rest and refill?
How? When? Where?

27

SEASONS OF WORSHIP I MICKEY MANGUN

Mickey Mangun has been at the forefront of worship ministry, touching lives from every facet of society. Whether leading worship at The Pentecostals of Alexandria, LA, singing before Governors and Presidents, or simply singing a "going home" song to a dying saint, she epitomizes a woman of God with a heart of worship.

To every thing there is a season,
and a time to every purpose under the heaven...
(Ecclesiastes 3:1-8) KJV

The writer of Ecclesiastes, that man of great wisdom, had a keen insight into a very basic principle of life - our days being measured in seasons and the very basic human need for purpose. *"To every thing there is a season; and a time to every purpose..."*

We all have a basic understanding of seasons and often refer to the four seasons of winter, spring, summer, and fall. That's what most of us experience every year. In Minnesota, Iowa, and Missouri, where I spent my early years – winters were hard and long and snow was inevitable. The other three seasons seemed to speed by and never last long enough. Moving south to Arkansas, Texas and eventually Louisiana, it became the summer season that seemed endless and now winter may only last a few days or weeks at the most.

It's interesting to note that in the area of the world where the original text was penned, there are basically only two seasons: winter and summer. A travel website notes: "The weather in Jerusalem is usually very predictable. There are two distinct seasons in the center of Israel: winter and summer. In between, we're graced with a few delightful weeks of spring."

So, as in the seasons of life . . .there are seasons of worship. Sometimes you may find yourself progressing through all four – and very distinct ones at that. At other times, you may feel you alternate between the frigid snowy days of winter and the stifling heat of summer. And other times, like the songwriter for the group Unspoken penned, it seems like *four seasons of winter."*

There are seasons when it's war time and worship becomes a battle cry. There are other times when worship is soaked in tears and moments are tender. There are the dry, desert seasons when the heart cries for the water of worship. There are the brilliants days of spring, when the season seems to call for a worship celebration. In the cold of winter, our souls seek the warmth of His presence in worship. In the heat of summer or the labor of fall, we seek seasons of rest and restoration. In seasons of chaos, our worship brings peace. In seasons of trouble and loss, there is the comfort of worship. In seasons of triumph, the worship songs of victory spring forth.

Whatever the season, it is a season of worship . . . and then there's the rest of the verse. . . "...A time to every purpose . . . "

In the presence and posture of true worship, whatever the season, we can discover the time and purpose of where we are and who we are. The things of life that consume so much of our time and energy are, for the most part, temporal, not eternal. Worship brings things into focus. It allows us to catch a glimpse of God's perspective, as well as re-focusing us on the reason for our season of life.

Worship can convict us; worship can affirm us; worship can call us and it does. Whatever the season, it is the season to worship. We have been called to worship and therein discover His purpose for each of us in this world.

HEART QUESTIONS TO PONDER:

What season of worship is a "good season" for you?

What season do you look forward to? What season do you dread?

What season are you in? What season is coming?
Are you prepared?

29

PROPHETIC PARADOX I DEREK CRADDOCK

Derek is a passionate minister of music who gives God a spirit of excellence in all he does. He is the Now Generation leader for Heart of Worship and serves at Northgate Pentecostals in Ft. Worth, TX.

> *When Mary came to the place where Jesus was and saw Him,*
> *she dropped down at His feet, saying to Him,*
> *if You had been here, my brother would not have died.*
> *When Jesus saw her sobbing,*
> *and the Jews who came with her [also] sobbing,*
> *He was deeply moved in spirit and troubled...*
>
> *But some of them said, Could not He*
> *Who opened a blind man's eyes*
> *have prevented this man from dying?*
> *(John 11:33,37) AMPC*

In today's society, we seem to be governed solely by our emotional response to what we see and feel. Oftentimes our actions are based not on our spiritual beliefs in God's power, but by how a situation can be controlled using our own abilities. Even when God has spoken a prophetic word directly into our spirits, our urgency to pray, fast, and read the Word suddenly becomes a technique to govern our situation, rather than to glorify the One who has already spoken it into existence.

How do we respond when what we see with our physical eye is contradictory to the promises of God? Do we follow Him to the tomb where our promise lies, or do we give in to the inner voice of doubt and unbelief? Will we allow a prophetic paradox to rob us of our spiritual moment with the Messiah?

Consider the words of Jon Acuff:

> "if someone talked to you the way you talk to you,
> you wouldn't get coffee with them.
> You'd tell them they were really discouraging and hurtful.
> You'd wonder why he doubts on your dreams so much."

If we allow the circumstance in our view to dictate our every thought, we prioritize the problem, subconsciously creating an idol in our spiritual walk with God. Listening to the voice of self can be the greatest hindrance in seeing a promise come to fruition. Even though Jesus spoke earlier in John 11 that "Lazarus' illness will not lead to death," Lazarus was still buried in a tomb.

Much like this passage, we are inclined to lean into things we can only measure with our physical eye. Even though Jesus spoke the promise, Lazarus was now dead and Jesus is nowhere to be found.

Could Jesus have healed him instantly, or made his way to Lazarus with haste? Of course. He's God. He can do anything! I believe when you consider His affection towards this family, He intentionally delayed, so a greater purpose could come to pass. He planned to do something extraordinary for them, to work a unique miracle. Perhaps if Christ had come sooner and healed Lazarus before he died, it would have been a miracle no greater than he did for someone else. However, through this delay, Mary and Martha gained a greater understanding of the love and affection of Christ. And Jesus brought honor and glory to Himself.

Waiting on a promise can be a difficult task when you're leaning on your own strength. Much like Martha, we understand God has the power to fulfill what He said, but we lack the faith to sustain us in the process. Martha's lack of faith hindered her ability to believe

God for the impossible. If in the moment you feel like God is far away from you, take notice of verse 35. *"Jesus wept."* In that moment the outcome could have been distinctly different, but yet the God of the universe knew exactly how they felt. He understood the pain and sorrow of death as they made their way to the tomb of Lazarus. Trust that God sees you in this moment and He can carry you. Understand that though your promise looks dead, in the end, that promise wrapped in grave clothes will live again!

By silencing our inner voice of doubt and unbelief, we can combat what we see with our physical eye in light of what God has promised. If we can take solace in the fact that God's promises are *yes* (2 Corinthians 1:20), we can overcome any obstacle in our way. His Word is worth following even when it appears to be an utter paradox.

HEART QUESTIONS TO PONDER:

Consider the John Acuff quote. Do I have a tendency to speak negatively over my promises?

Do I have a promise God has given me that seems paradoxically unanswered? If so, how can I begin to speak life over it today?

29

CELEBRATING THROUGH LAMENT I
BETSY RUVALCABA-CHRISTENSEN

*Betsy came to the US from Mexico as a young woman; Spanish is her
native tongue. Her passion for worship is infectious! She has been used
mightily in both English and Spanish worship environments. She is a
licensed minister.*

> *How long, O Lord? Will You forget me forever?*
> *How long will You hide Your face from me?*
> *How long shall I take counsel in my soul,*
> *Having sorrow in my heart daily?*
> *How long will my enemy be exalted over me?*
> Psalm 13:1-2 NKJV

I've been writing in journals since I was 14 years old; these are my
prayers to the Lord. Every event, emotion, feeling, desire and
longing is carefully recorded in every page. A few weeks ago I
looked over the pages of the past 12 years and read each page.
You can imagine what I found: Life. Seasons of life. Spring.
Summer. Fall. And, more recently, a very long winter...

As I read through the pages of "my winter," I saw evidence of my
rollercoaster of emotions. Despair and tragedy intermingled with
prayers of sorrow, supplication, faith and hope. I felt sadness
overwhelming my heart, and I thought,

*My goodness, that's so depressing! Why did you write all these bad
things? You should have only written the good stuff!*

Yet after a time of sadness, my heart suddenly shifted to overflowing joy! Sadness with joy? Yes! What an oxymoron! You see, if I had not written the negative I would not have been able to see how faithful God has been. Reading back, I see my faith was tested in the storm, and now understand how the hand of the Lord kept me and pulled me through it all.

I can still feel the cries of my soul to the Lord as I read through some pages. But I know this. When I walked in the dark and my song was sung in a minor key, His promises were still true and unshakable. Honestly, confessing my own frailty, inabilities, and struggles to the Lord opened up a straight way to the throne room. In this path of faith, although my circumstances dictated the opposite, my soul knew very well from where my help would come.

Lament is a seldom-practiced form of worship. It expresses the raw, sensitive, and unadulterated frailty of humanity in contrast with the amazing attributes of my God who understands, loves and cares for his creation. Laments in Scripture include a specific complaint, a confession of trust, a prayer for deliverance followed by a praise and thanksgiving in faith for the answer to our lament.

It is not God's will for us to hold our grief, suffering, pain and struggles. We can come to our loving God who is *"a man of sorrows, acquainted with deepest grief…"* (Isaiah 53:3) NLT and pour out our hearts in His presence. Through our lament we glorify God, we are strengthened in our faith, we deepen our relationship with Him, and we truly learn to trust.

Laments are the expression of our "winters" and are necessary in our lives. Winters are what make our fruit have weight. In winter a tree draws all the nutrients it can from its roots. The better the ground, the better the fruit and the more nutrients it will receive. If a tree is planted in shallow ground, a heavy winter will knock it down. There are no nutrients for it to sustain itself. If a tree is removed from one ground to another to avoid a necessary winter, it will either damage its fruit forever, or be its demise. Pour out your heart in lament to the Lord during your winter, stand firm and grounded, knowing spring is coming soon!

Why all these confusions and pain my God?
Why is there a falling star?
Why must leaves fall and crash without a cry?
Why snow on a sunny day?
Why clouds before the light?

But You alone are sovereign God,
Please help me understand
That there's no victory without a battle,
No joy without sorrow,
No healing without pain
No grace without an empty grave!

So I choose to rejoice in the middle of my pain.
I trust You, my Lord although I don't understand.
I celebrate Your goodness that follows me everyday
For You alone are God and in You alone I stand!

(Journal of Betsy Ruvalcaba-Christensen 2014)

Express your situation to the Lord and celebrate His faithfulness through your very own "Lament". Make sure you include the vital elements of complaint, confession of trust, prayer for deliverance and praise and thanksgiving in faith for your answer.

HEART QUESTIONS TO PONDER:

Am I allowing myself to be planted in good ground so my roots can be properly nourished and I endure through the "winters" of life?

Do I often struggle to see the spiritual value of lament and push myself and others around me to just "be happy?"

What can I do differently as a worship leader to implement the lost practice of lament in my congregation?

30

LEARNING TO WORSHIP AGAIN I KRISTIE KOBZEFF

Kristie is a worshiper and a prayer warrior. She serves faithfully in ministry and her outstanding organizational abilities are currently being put to good use at the North American Missions department of the United Pentecostal Church international.

> *I will bless the Lord at all times;*
> *His praise shall continually be in my mouth.*
> *Psalms 34:1(NKJV)*

> *It is good to give thanks to the Lord,*
> *And to sing praises to Your name, O Most High;*
> *To declare Your lovingkindness in the morning,*
> *And your faithfulness every night...*
> *Psalms 92:1, 2 (NKJV)*

Isn't it easy to worship and sing praises when things are sunny outside, and life is grand? What about the times, though, when the storm clouds come, and the thunder and lightning strike out the sunny skies? When storms come into our lives, we may have a hard time worshiping. We may feel isolated, alone, afraid, intimidated, and even angry.

A storm is any disturbed state of an environment or astronomical body's atmosphere, especially affecting its surface, and strongly implying severe weather. It may be marked by significant disruptions to normal conditions. Storms generally lead to negative impacts on lives and property.

Now let's talk about storms that are personal... and I'm not talking about the weather.

A severe storm of lies, betrayal, and deceit crept into my home. I had never experienced the feeling of rejection and then abandonment as I did during that season. At that time, I did not realize that depression was so close to overtaking my life. I was able to smile on the outside, but on the inside my heart was slowly breaking. I was numb and began to build a thick wall of protection around my heart. I almost lost my praise, yet in the darkest of nights, I learned:

> *God is our refuge and strength,*
> *a very present help in trouble*
> Psalms 46:1 (NKJV)

In the most trying time of my life, I discovered:

> *The Lord is my light and my salvation;*
> *whom shall I fear?*
> *The Lord is the strength of my life;*
> *of whom shall I be afraid?*
> Psalms 27:1 (NKJV)

> *The Lord is my rock and my fortress*
> *and my deliverer; my God, my strength,*
> *in whom I will trust; my shield*
> *and the horn of my salvation, my stronghold.*
> Psalms 18:2 (NKJV)

During this severe storm, I learned a few things. I was able to "bless the Lord" at all times, and continue to worship Him through the storms, because I had confidence that He would always take care of me. No matter how dark it was, God was always brighter. No matter how strong the turbulence was, God was always my shelter. He was the constant in my life. He was my provider. He never left me. He never forgot about me. He really did care about me.

> I call to remembrance my song in the night;
> I meditate within my heart,
> and my spirit makes diligent search.
> (Psalms 77:6) NKJV

> "Any fool can sing in the day.
> It's easy to sing when we can read the notes by daylight.
> But the skillful singer is the one who can sing
> when there is not a ray of light to read by.
> Songs in the night come only from God.
> They are not in the power of man."
> C.H. Spurgeon

Remember storms are only for a season. The very same God who spoke into the darkest of voids and said, "Let there be light," will one day speak into the darkness of your life and you will be able to worship through it all. You will be able to sing a joyful song again. You will be able to worship again.

When you are battling storms of your own, here are some suggestions to help you continue to worship in spite of the storm:

1. Worship the Creator

> Enter into His gates with thanksgiving,
> and into His courts with praise.
> Be thankful to Him and bless His name.
> (Psalms 100:4) NKJV

2. Listen to uplifting music and preaching

You have turned my mourning into joyful dancing.
You have taken away my clothes of mourning and clothed me
with joy, that I might sing praises to you and not be silent.
O LORD my God, I will give thanks forever!
(Psalms 30:11-12) NLT

HEART QUESTIONS TO PONDER:

Am I feeding my spirit with things that lift my focus out of
my storm?

What can I do to keep worshipping through the storm?

What has God revealed to me about Himself through the dark
seasons of life?

A FINAL CHALLENGE: WORSHIP TOGETHER

31

KINGDOM COMMUNITY | LAURA PAYNE

Laura is the founder of Heart of Worship Ministries, the Choral Director Director for Urshan College as well as a Licensed Minister. Laura's passion for mentoring worshipers is evident through the lives she has touched around the globe.

> *For just as we have many members in one body*
> *and all the members*
> *do not have the same function,*
> *so we, who are many, are one body in Christ,*
> *and individually members one of another.*
> *(Romans 12:4-5) ESV*

When I was growing up, my most meaningful musical moments happened in our family room, as I sat at a black Swedish upright piano. I'd shut the door and turn on the brass piano light with the crooked neck so that a small beam of aged-yellow light shone on the keys. In my private corner of the house, I'd sing and play for God alone. I loved the solitude. And I believed that my greatest God-connections would happen in dimly lit, lonely spaces such as this one.

As I've grown older, my favorite God-moments have changed. Now, my best memories with God always include others. I've realized that whether it's in worship, in planning, in celebrating, in stage design, in administrative work, in prayer or just in living life, God is dwelling in the midst of my healthy Kingdom relationships. Now I crave the beauty of these collaborative moments. My eyes see more of the greatness of God because I am surrounding myself with others who are pursuing His Kingdom with me.

There's a powerful scripture that we often misunderstand because of the limitations of the English language:

> *Know YE not that YE are the temple of God,*
> *and that the Spirit of God dwelleth in YOU?*
> (I Corinthians 3:16) KJV

Like I did, I'm sure you've interpreted it this way in your head for years:

> *You, hey you over there!*
> *Yes, you, sitting alone in your family room*
> *under the small light cast by a brass light.*
> *YOU are the temple of God!*

But that's not at all what the scripture means. Because *"you"* in this passage is a second-person plural pronoun. It means:

> *You ALL are the temple of God!*
> *His spirit dwells in you when*
> *YOU are collectively together.*
> *Engaging one another.*

God created His body with unique members. He challenges this unique collection of gifts and talents and personalities to be jointly fit together, because He understood that we would always be greater together than we could be alone. It is the will and intention of our creator that we "do" life together in *Kingdom Community*. It's a big revelation to see how God more perfectly dwells in US than He does in ME.

> *For where two or three are gathered*
> *together as my followers,*
> *I am there among them.*
> (Matthew 18:20) NLT

Music and worship are a great place to see this Kingdom principle in action. A bass player alone only has so much value. Yet when we put him in the band, with a few other musicians, his value increases exponentially. One soprano is a blessing, but a choir of anointed singers can transform a room. However, so many times in the local church we do music together, then our kingdom connection stops when the song ends.

It is the enemy of our soul that causes us to sink into isolation. Things like a critical spirit, perfectionism and competition can easily plague the music department. These qualities creep into worshipers and send us to our homes feeling lonely and disconnected from one another, rather than allowing us to feel strengthened by the joy of being jointly fit together.

There's nothing as beautiful and encouraging as living in *Kingdom Community*. My community has the spiritual strength to pray me over mountains. My community has my permission to challenge my mediocre thoughts. My community has wisdom to guide me through tough decisions. And the arms of my community reach to pull me up when I feel I'm drowning in my own daily grind.

Here's the truth. No one of us has our act completely together. We cannot build a masterful temple for the glory of God without leaning on the strengths and gifts of one another. Everything beautiful I do in life will be because I have yoked myself together with other precious servants of God who have been uniquely positioned by my side.

HEART QUESTIONS TO PONDER:

Do I have any rough edges that make it difficult for me to be "jointly fit together" with the church family God has given to me?

What have I been trying to do on my own
that I should do with someone else?

In what ways do I see the beauty of God in the
Kingdom Community He's given me?

REFERENCES

Wonder

Tripp, P.D. (2015). *Awe: Why it Matters for Everything We Think, Say, and Do.* Crossway.

Boberg, C. (1885). How Great Thou Art. Public Domain.

Guarding Our Landmarks

McLeod, S. (2008). *Ash Experiment.* from

https://www.cbsd.org/cms/lib/PA01916442/Centricity/Domain/2773/com

monlit_asch-experiment_student.pdf

Bring Me A Minstrel

Gaither, B. (1963) He Touched Me. Brentwood-Benson Music / Gaither

Copyright management.

Confronting Insecurities

Insecurity {Def.1-5}. (n.d.) In *Miriam Webster Online.* Retrieved November

2019, from

https://www.merriamwebster.com/?utm_source=google&utm_campaign=

dictionary&utm_medium=cpc&gclid=EAIaIQobChMI1MLq1rjw6AIVOv3jB

x0IYQJwEAAYASAAEgJLtPD_BwE.

Power in Surrender

Taylor, H. and Roberts, J. (2104). *Learning to Let Go.* James Roberts

Music.

Leadership Through Servanthood

DuPré Pesmen, P. (Producer), Hicks, A, Jones, R. (Director). (2018). *Quincy.*

United States: TriBeCa Productions.

The "Why" of Excellence
Sinek, S. (2009). *Start With Why*. Penguin Group.

Worship and our Relationship with Jesus
Redman, M. (1997). *Heart of Worship*. Thankyou Music.

Seasons of Worship
Rich, M. (2019) Unspoken Reason. Retrieved October 2019.
https://todayschristianent.com/unspoken-reason/

Redman, M. (1997). *Heart of Worship*. Thankyou Music.

_____ Retrieved October 2019. https://www.jerusalem-insiders-guide.com/weather-in-jerusalem.html.

Prophetic Paradox
Acuff, J. (2019). from https://acuff.me/2013/11/1-person-need-ignore.

Learning to Worship Again
Spurgeon, C.H. (2007). *Sermons of the Rev. C.H. Spurgeon of London.* Kessinger Publishing.

Heart of Worship Ministries is committed to
strengthening worshipers across the globe.
We pray that our honest, personal stories and devotional thoughts
have spoken inspiration to you.

We'd love to hear your feedback at
admin@theheartofworship.net

Made in the USA
Monee, IL
05 August 2023

40480535R00088